HOT TIPS
for the
HOME
RECORDING
STUDIO

HOT TIPS for the HOME RECORDING STUDIO

Hank Linderman

WRITER'S DIGEST BOOKS

Cincinnati, Ohio

This hardcover edition of *Hot Tips for the Home Recording Studio* features a "self-jacket" that eliminates the need for a separate dust jacket. It provides sturdy protection for your book while it saves paper, trees and energy.

98 97 96 95 94   5 4 3 2 1

Library of Congress Cataloging-in-Publication Data

Linderman, Hank
   Hot tips for the home recording studio / Hank Linderman.
     p.   cm.
  Includes index.
  ISBN 0-89879-651-2
  1. Sound—recording and reproducing. 2. Sound studios. I. Title.
TK7881.4.L54 1994
781.49—dc20   94-22261
                                                  CIP

Edited by Mark Garvey
Interior design by Brian Roeth
Cover design by Clare Finney

ACKNOWLEDGMENTS

I would like to thank John Braheny at the Los Angeles Songwriter's Showcase — who knew that, when he agreed to let me write a column for the LASS "Musepaper," I'd get offered a book deal. Thanks also to John's partner, Len Chandler. Together they have made the difference for hundreds (thousands?) of songwriters in Los Angeles. Another major resource for songwriters in Los Angeles is K.A. Parker. I'm proud to be an alumnus of her Sunday night songwriting workshops.

Many friends have helped me to improve, by providing me with opportunities and knowledge. In no particular order (and I'm sure I've forgotten several of them — sorry), thanks to Steve Levine, Gerry Beckley, Dewey Bunnell, Chip Davis, Walker Igleheart, Hill Tigay, Bob Ramsey, Mark Holden, Annamarie Stanton, Erik Andrews, Jan Linder, Tom Lerner, Geoff Aymar, Chris Dixon, Ron Fin, Parker McGee, Jamie Houston, Yale Beebee, Karen Hart, Ron Dabs, Greg Laney, Shakeh Herbekian, Marty Rifkin, Jennifer Holt, Hugh James, Cecil and Stacie Womack, Dave Morgan, Jack Wessell, Alan O'Day and Kyle Vincent.

In the business, thanks to my friends Paige Sober at BMI, Brendan Okrent at ASCAP, and Tony Gottlieb at Morningstar. Also, thanks to Kenny Dewees at Far Out Music in Jeffersonville, Indiana; Marvin Maxwell at Mom's Music in Louisville, Kentucky; and Mark Bookin, Keith Winston and Fred Walecki at Westwood Music, Westwood, California. (These guys give the best deals — just tell them you're a friend of mine. . . .)

Special thanks to my editors, Mandi Martin-Fox at LASS (overworked and underpaid, but greatly appreciated) and Mark Garvey at Writer's Digest books. Thanks to both of you for your encouragement. Mark, thanks so much for the opportunity to write this book — I never knew I had it in me.

Finally, thanks to my wife Pam and my daughters Maggie and Lucy; they continue to put up with all the guitar cases, the computers, the cables, the noise. . . .

ABOUT THE AUTHOR

Hank Linderman is a songwriter, producer and guitarist who has worked in the Los Angeles area since 1983. He has written the column "Tools of the Trade" in the Los Angeles Songwriter's Showcase "Musepaper" for several years, and has produced hundreds of demos for local songwriters and artists. He recently completed work as assistant producer and guitarist with the band America on their album *Hourglass* for American Gramaphone Records. He lives in Santa Monica with his wife, Pam, and daughters Maggie and Lucy.

PREFACE

I have to confess, I'm not a very organized person. When the offer to write this book came, I was excited and flattered. Once I'd made the commitment, I realized I'd actually have to write the thing! This was a rude awakening, since it meant that I'd have to organize my thoughts about making demos better than I ever had.

I've made lots of demos, for myself and for others, and I had always sort of wandered through the process, facing each challenge as it came. (As my friend Steve Levine says, "Production is problem solving.") Over the course of these demos, I've run into lots of problems to solve, and the results are in this book. I want to warn you that the answers I've found won't work 100 percent of the time for you (they don't work 100 percent of the time for me), but I hope they'll get you thinking in a helpful direction.

I also want to encourage you to jump from section to section, rather than read the book from front to back. For example, the first section, "Equipment and Technology," won't be very useful to you if you've already got a firm grasp of the mechanics involved. Before I started writing, I wanted this book to be the type that one could simply open to almost any page and begin reading: Since the process of making demos is so open-ended, I wanted the book to be the same. If, however, you do want to read this book from top to bottom, go ahead. Hopefully I became organized enough to satisfy you! Thanks for reading, and happy demo making.

INTRODUCTION

FIRST, A LITTLE PHILOSOPHY

Making demos is a fairly complicated task; there are lots of techniques to master, and new techniques (and technologies) are added on a regular basis. I'm always bumping into some new thing I need to learn or finding that what I already knew is now outdated. For this reason, I've found that having a good philosophical approach is more important than any technical knowledge I have: Technical knowledge constantly shifts, but a good philosophical approach remains stable.

So, we need a little philosophy before we get started making demos. I've hinted at a first point. You'd better be prepared to . . .

Keep Learning

I've never stopped learning about recording. Because the job involves so many procedures and because there are so many tools to use, you should be prepared to keep abreast of the latest developments. You may not be able to use more than half of what you know, but the day will come when you are the hero because you knew a way out of a particular mess. I read magazines that cover recording and producing, I listen to new (and old) recordings looking for production ideas, and I talk to other people involved in recording — this is my ongoing learning process. Other people are an especially good source for new techniques and approaches. I have a habit of looking and listening very closely when I work with someone else. I tell myself, "Everyone does something really well — what trick does this person have?" If I'm able to see someone do his "trick," I can usually learn how to do it, or at least be made aware that it can be done!

Passion Versus Perfection

This is one of the age-old problems of art, and indeed, life. If you can learn to balance these two incompatible goals, you'll be most of the way home. Here's what I've found: You've got to have some technique before you start creating. Even if you start with passion, you won't be able to play guitar until you develop some rudimentary technique — it makes no matter that you use a sledgehammer instead of a pick; it's still technique. So, develop some technique before you get too deep into writing, recording, cooking, whatever. As you develop your technique, keep your passion alive by applying it to the techniques you've learned. I forget where I heard it, but a musician once told me, "Practice in the daytime, jam at night."

As you learn more and more technique, you'll find that your skills become "invisible" in the recording process. When I'm recording a vocal, I don't have to think about punching in, I just do it — the process is invisible. This makes whoever is singing more able to concentrate on simply singing, especially if I'm the singer.

All of this having been said, there will be occasions when your technique or your tools are not up to the job at hand. Maybe you haven't had time to set the vocal mic properly, or you just don't have the ideal tools. In this case, you must sacrifice technique for passion. Don't let the performance get away! (*Always* record the first take. More on this later.) Even if it's a little distorted, or you're using the wrong mic, or you can hear the cars on the street driving by on the tape, record it! A passionate performance with some technical problems is much more listenable and valuable than a perfectly recorded but passionless take.

Develop Your Intuition

I had to look this up — "Intuition: 1. a. The act or faculty of knowing without the rational process; immediate cognition; b. Knowledge so gained; a sense of something not evident or deducible; 2. A capacity for guessing accurately." (From *The American Heritage Dictionary of the English Language*, New College Edition)

Your intuition is an invaluable tool in the recording process. There will be hundreds of decisions you need to make, and your intuition can be a helpful guide. How can you develop your intuition? First, realize that everyone has intuition in varying degrees and that everyone can increase their sensitivity to their own intuition. That's really the main secret — becoming more sensitive to that little voice in your head that says things like, "Something's wrong here," or, "*That* was really cool. . . ." The voice in your head is usually very quiet and extremely easy to ignore, so try to get in the habit of paying close attention anytime you hear it. Also, be aware that intuition, like any of your senses, is not 100 percent accurate. It's just another source of information for you to use, or not.

Creativity

One of the joys of working on demos is being able to use your creativity. At every step, you are likely to come face to face with a new situation that requires a new approach, so creativity must be encouraged. It may help for you to use a three-step approach to problem solving. Step one: Idea generation. Come up with as many ideas as you can *without judging them*. Get everyone involved, and don't stop until you've exhausted the possibilities. Step two: Judging the ideas. Decide on the best approaches to the problem at hand, and select the first one to try. Step three: Implementation. Do it! If the first solution doesn't work, try another.

You'll notice that a good recording atmosphere is required if creativity is to be encouraged.

The Recording Atmosphere

I love analogies. My favorite analogy for the recording process is playing with a beach ball. The object of the game is to keep the ball floating for as long as possible—I'll hit it to you, you hit it to her, she hits it back to you, you hit it to me, etc. As long as we all work together and keep our eyes on the ball, we do fine and have a good time while we're doing it.

I think of the music as being the beach ball. We have to keep the music "floating," and it doesn't matter whose turn it is, we all lose (temporarily) if the beach ball lands on the ground.

This positive environment is threatened when someone takes his eyes off the ball and begins to concentrate on himself, focusing on what he wants and how he's doing. At this point, the game has changed from keeping the ball in the air to keeping track of who is doing the most and deserves the most credit. So much for having fun.

I'm not saying that there shouldn't be someone in charge in the studio. What I'm saying is that if all participants do their own jobs in a helpful fashion, keeping eyes on the ball, the recording process is enhanced.

This analogy applies to ideas, too. Even if it's your song, you should be willing to consider other people's ideas, particularly when they are coming from someone you brought into the studio with you. Shame on you if you're one of those who only care about her own ideas! If this is you, then you haven't been keeping your eyes on the ball. I've been around only a few of this type of person, and they were without exception among the least creative people I've worked with—they were too threatened by someone else's ideas and too concerned about getting their way to be creative. The most creative people I've been involved with are always ready to hear ideas, even if they use very few of them.

Useful Communication

Obviously, communication in the studio should be friendly and cooperative, but it must also be useful! Useful communication is honest and specific. What good is it to be told about your performance: "I don't know, it just doesn't sound right. . . ." Wouldn't you rather hear something like: "The *I love you* was great, but the *baby* was flat. Try it one more time"; or, "The first four measures of your solo were great, but the last four need to get into a higher range. I'll punch you in at measure five."

Doing Your Best

Sounds obvious, doesn't it? Always do your best. The problem comes in doing your best after eight hours in a session. It gets tempting to take shortcuts, like not cleaning the tape machine, or not being as careful about sounds you're working on. Resist the temptation! If you're serious about your demos, remember that each one is a roving representative of your work. Do you want something that's less than your best floating around?

By the way, always doing your best doesn't mean always doing your absolute best. Olympic gold medalists don't function at gold-medal levels every day. Do the best you are capable of on that day, in that situation. That's all you can ask of yourself.

Learning the Rules, and Breaking Them

Every rule is meant to be broken. There's very little I can tell you that works 100 percent of the time, so don't feel bound by the rules. This doesn't mean you can get by not learning the rules—that's simply laziness. Learn the rules (techniques), find what works for you, and be prepared to change any of it.

Some of the suggestions I make might be contrary to the way you've done things for years. If so, great! (Let me know about your way of doing something—I'd love to try it.)

There's No Particular Order to This Process

One reason that doing demos can be so complicated is that there's no set order to the process. (I've chosen an order for this book for the purpose of illustration. Feel free to modify as your situation requires.) Some demos start with a sequencer and end with a lead vocal; others start with the lead vocal and end with the sequencer. If you're locked into "only one way to do a demo," you need to learn some more technique. Hopefully, you'll find those new techniques here.

You're Gonna Pay

Here's the bad news: It costs money to make demos, and you're gonna' pay, one way or the other. If you buy the equipment yourself and learn to operate it, you can save money, especially if you do lots of demos. This book is filled with tips that will help you make better demos and speed up your process, thereby gaining more for your money in less time. Then again, if you are a songwriter who would rather write more songs than wrestle with a computer or a tape machine, or if you simply don't want to twist knobs, it makes much more sense for you to find someone like me to produce your demos. If you are this person, this book will help you communicate what you want to the producer.

There are many ways to save money on demos, and I'll point these things out from time to time, but the biggest way to save money is to be prepared before the session. The most expensive way to do a demo is to have extended decision-making sessions at the studio. Besides, you shouldn't compromise too much by insisting that everything be cheap. This diagram should explain what I mean:

GOOD

CHEAP   FAST

(choose any two)

PART ONE

EQUIPMENT AND TECHNOLOGY

MIXER BASICS

When people come into my studio, the first thing they see is my mixing console. "How do you know what to do with all those knobs?" is the standard question I get. Knowing what to do with all those knobs is exactly the job when it comes to getting the most out of your mixer. Every sound on your tapes goes through your mixer, so you'd better know how to use it. This section will be a bit technical, but stick with me: The only way to make great demos is to know how to use your mixer.

Your mixer has a huge effect on how your recordings will sound, as much as any other piece in your studio. In fact, with the advent of very low noise digital recorders like the Alesis ADAT and the Tascam Hi-8, the console has become one of the major sources of noise in the recording process. If you use good microphones and a good tape recorder with a lousy mixing console (or if you use a good mixer with lousy technique), the results will show. What is a good mixer? To me, first and foremost is sound quality, particularly in the areas of noise and distortion. Another aspect of sound quality is the equalization capability of the mixer. The additional important feature to look for is flexibility—how many channels, how many sends, how many insert points, etc.

Flexibility is important because each recording session is unique unto itself—each session invariably presents new problems. When those problems involve the routing of various sounds, a flexible mixer makes all the difference.

Even if you've got a good mixer, you really need to know how to operate it properly in order to get the quality of sound the specifications sheet promises. The key to understanding what to do with all the knobs is to realize that there is lots of duplication, even in the largest recording consoles. Once you've got a handle on one input channel, for example, you understand all twelve, sixteen, twenty-four, or however many channels you've got. You'll also find that the bulk of your work on a mixer is done at the input modules, so it's important to develop as much expertise with the inputs as possible. Let's start by looking at one input channel of a fairly involved console—mine.

The Input Channel

The input section performs the following functions: selection of the sound source (tape/mic/line); adjustment of the preamp level (a very important and overlooked function); equalization; effects sends; panning and assignment; and fader level. All these functions are controlled by switches and pots and a fader. There is another section of the input module — the actual inputs! These are the jacks where you plug in your sources (tape/mic/line) and often where you can "insert" an effect or other processor that will be used only on that particular channel.

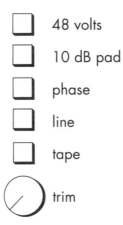

48 volts

10 dB pad

phase

line

tape

trim

Preamp

Here's the first section of the input module, and it's found at the top of the channel. The first switch selects phantom power for condenser microphones — leave this switch off if you're using a dynamic mic or other "unpowered" source. Switch two puts a 10 dB pad (turns the gain down by 10 dB) on the mic input. The pad works in conjunction with the "trim" pot, to adjust the level of the mic before it goes any further through the input.

Switch three reverses the phase of whichever signal is selected (tape/mic/line): this switch is used when using several mics at once, such as miking a drum set. It reverses the electrical polarity (positive becomes negative, negative becomes positive) to compensate for acoustic phase differences. Another use might be when using two different samples to make one sound — if the samples are out of phase, you can reverse one of them. How can you tell when sounds are out of phase? Try this experiment: Connect a stereo source (CD player, stereo synth) to two inputs, and listen. Next, switch the phase of *one* of the inputs. Hear the difference? You should be hearing tonal and spatial (the stereo image) changes. Now, switch the phase of the second input. The sound should be back to normal. Repeat this experiment with your mixer set to mono (or with the two inputs panned to the center, instead of left/right). You should notice some extreme tonal differences. All of this points out just how important phase is. Fortunately, you won't have to deal with phase problems very often, but it's nice to have the capability.

The next two switches select between the sources. The way my mixer works is that if the "tape" switch is selected, then the position of the "line" switch doesn't matter; in other words, "tape" has priority over the other inputs. When "tape" is not selected, the "line" switch selects between line and mic inputs.

The final control in this first group is the "trim" adjustment, and it's probably the most important adjustment to be made on your mixer. The reason I say this is that if the trim is set improperly, nothing can be done to correct the problems that will show up. The two problems you'll find are our old friends, noise and distortion. When a signal enters the mixer, the first thing that happens is that it is sent to the pad and trim control. Since the levels of different signals will vary quite a bit, the pad and trim are provided for you to match the incoming level to the rest of the input module. If the incoming level is quiet, you'll need to adjust the trim higher; if the incoming level is very loud, you'll need to turn the trim down. (If you're using a mic on a very loud source, turning the trim down all the way may not be enough. In this case, simply select the 10 dB pad. You may have to turn the trim back up a little bit to find the optimum level. Notice that the pad works on mic only.)

What is the optimum level? Simply, it's the level at which noise and distortion are minimized. There are a few techniques you'll need to learn. Number one is to use your ears. Turn the trim pad all of the way up and listen to your source without any equalization. (Be sure to keep your monitor volume down so you don't damage your ears or your speakers.) If the source is hot enough, you should be hearing distortion, and if your input has a "clip" indicator (usually a red light), you should be getting visual feedback that distortion is occurring. Listen to the distortion, and begin turning the trim pot down. If you need to, you can also adjust your monitor level up as you turn the trim down, so you won't be confused by the level changes that will be occurring right along with the distortion changes. Once your ears tell you that the distortion has gone, notice the position of the trim pot. Continue lowering the level of the trim and adjusting the monitor level up. Notice anything? You should be hearing the noise level climbing, first hiss, then hum. If you continue to ridiculous extremes, you'll be hearing more noise than signal. You can now reset the trim to the level where you stopped hearing distortion.

Using your ears is the best way to set the trim, although it's also helpful to have visual indications, like the "clip" light. Meters are helpful too, particularly if you have a "solo" function on your meter. While you're listening to set the trim, you can solo the channel and view the input level on a meter. When the meter shows about +3 dB at the loudest levels and the clip indicator only occasionally starts to flicker, you've probably got the levels sorted out. Bear in mind that all mixers and meters are different, so trust your ears most of all.

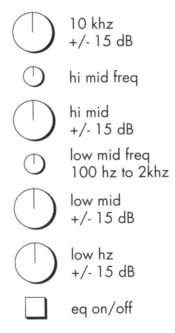

10 khz
+/- 15 dB

hi mid freq

hi mid
+/- 15 dB

low mid freq
100 hz to 2khz

low mid
+/- 15 dB

low hz
+/- 15 dB

eq on/off

Equalizer section of input module

Equalizer
The next section of the input module is the equalizer. The example I'm using is a four-band equalizer, on which four different frequen-

cies can be adjusted at the same time. (For those of you who aren't aware of how frequency relates to sound, you need to know that the higher the frequency is, the higher the pitch will be. You also need to understand that as frequency doubles, pitch goes up one octave; therefore, the distance between 100 Hz and 200 Hz is an octave, as is the distance between 1000 Hz and 2000 Hz. By the way, 1000 Hz is also called 1 kilohertz, or 1 kHz.) The first band is for 10 kHz—very high frequency; if you set the knob for 6 dB of boost, you'll find that 10 kHz is louder by about 10 dB. Since this control is a *shelving* control (much like a treble or bass control on your stereo), it also affects the frequencies above 10 kHz. The other shelving type of control is in the fourth band—100 Hz. This control affects the low frequencies, and 6 dB of boost at 100 Hz will also affect the lower frequencies.

The two middle bands are a little more sophisticated. First, the middle bands have an extra control that lets you select which frequency the boost or cut knob will affect. Second, the boost/cut controls are *peaking* rather than shelving controls. This means that they will affect only the frequencies near the selected frequency. Try this experiment: Listen to a source with the low-mid control set to full boost. As you listen, rotate the frequency select control. Hear the boosted frequency sweep? Try the same thing with the high-mid control, and you'll hear a wah-wah effect. Next, try using full cut while you sweep the frequency selector. This should give you a phase-shifter effect.

The final control in this section is the eq on/off switch. In the *off* position the eq is removed from the channel circuit. You might wonder, What's the difference between setting the eq's boost/cut knobs to "flat" (12 o'clock: neither boosting nor cutting) and turning off the eq switch? The answer is that even with the eq set flat, the signal is going through unnecessary circuitry, which will add noise. Additionally, the flat setting of the knobs may not be 100 percent accurate. Another use for the eq on/off switch is a "preset" eq, such as a "megaphone" type of setting for a voice (boost at about 1 kHz and cut low and high eq—remember Rudy Valee!), that can be switched in at some point in a mix.

Effects Sends
The next section of the input module is the effects sends. Generally they all do the same thing—send your signal to a specific effect.

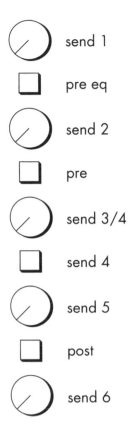

send 1

pre eq

send 2

pre

send 3/4

send 4

send 5

post

send 6

There are some differences you may run into, so it's a good idea to understand what's happening. The biggest variable you'll run into is whether the send is *pre-* or *post*fader. *Prefader* sends operate independently of the channel fader, and *postfader* sends are affected by the channel fader setting. Normally, *postfader* sends are preferred, since the relative amount of dry signal to effected signal will stay the same; fade the channel, and both the sound and the amount of the sound being sent to the effect are reduced. There are occasions when you'll need prefader sends, though, such as using the prefader send as a send for a separate headphone mix. This way, you can turn up any instrument the person using headphones wants without affecting the main monitor mix. Another use of a prefader send might be to allow separate fading of a sound without changing the effect; you could have the lead vocal fade away, while the lead vocal's reverb remains.

On the diagram above, notice that send one, which is normally postfader, can be made pre-eq. This means that the signal is sent to the effect before it is equalized; the eq settings will not affect the signal going out this send. Since the eq section of the input module is also prefader, selecting pre-eq also means that this send is a prefader send.

Send two allows you to select pre- or postfader. Sends three and four are postfader only, and are combined into one knob with a switch that selects which send is active. Only one of these two sends can be used by this channel at a time. This selector can also be used as a "preset" at mix time. If send three goes to a delay, and send four is not used (no effect is connected), you can switch the delay send for this input on and off by selecting between three and four.

Send five is normally prefader and can be switched to postfader. Send six is prefader only.

Panning, Fader and Channel Assignments
The final section of the input module includes panning, assignment and the channel fader. First is the pan knob. Rotating this knob from left to right will move the source from left to right within the stereo buss and from the odd assignment channels to the even. Notice all of the switches to the left of the fader—these are the assignment switches. Activating one of these switches will send the source to the appropriate outputs. This particular board has sixteen input modules and sixteen outputs, plus a stereo output. The assignment switches allow me to select where I want the signal to go. At mix time, for example, I almost always use the stereo buss (L/R) assignment for each channel, since the stereo outputs go to my mixdown machine. The pan knob lets me select where the source will appear, from left to right and anywhere in between.

During tracking, I listen to the channels through the stereo buss, with the exception of the channel providing the source I'm actually recording. In this instance, I'll use input 16 to mic an acoustic guitar. I've set the trim, adjusted the eq to my liking, and possibly connected a compressor at the channel insert point. While I could listen to the mic through the stereo buss, a better way exists. Let's assume that my sixteen outputs are assigned directly to my 16-track recorder, so that if I select 7/8 and set the pan left, the signal will go straight to channel 7 on my 16-track. If I then listen to channel 7, I can monitor what I'm recording while I'm doing it; then, during playback, I'll hear what ended up on tape. One thing to watch for

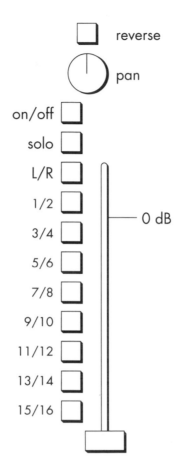

is assigning a tape channel back into itself, such as sending channel 7 to output 7. If you try to record on channel 7, you will probably get some serious feedback. How will you know if this happens? Believe me, everyone in the country will know from the noise that occurs. Hope your monitors don't blow. . . .

The beauty of using this arrangement is convenience. You can go from channel to channel recording your heart away without doing any more than throwing a few switches. It's logical, fast, easy, and . . . it doesn't sound as good as it could. The problem is that by using the output busses to send to your multitrack inputs, you've sent your signal through lots of extra circuitry that adds (you got it), noise and distortion. A better way is to take your signal out of the input module via the channel insert point. More on this a little later.

What are all of those output channels good for then, if you're just going to bypass them? For one thing, if you need to mix more than one source that will then be recorded on one track, you'll have to use one of the assignment busses. I do this all the time, such as using two or more synths to make a bass sound, which I then record on a single track. I can eq each sound separately—and add effects if I want—before assigning both to a buss for a particular channel on the 16-track. I also use cue mixes—a stereo mix that I can use as a reference to record additional tracks to. The standard time I do this is when I've got some sequenced tracks and it's time to record vocals or acoustic instruments. I make a stereo mix of my sequenced instruments and assign them to a pair of channels with the assignment buttons. Once the cue mix is recorded, I can turn off the computers, drum machines and synths, and record my vocals while I listen to the cue mix. The advantages of using the cue mix are that I don't have to worry about the MIDI stuff for awhile—waiting for the sequencer to "chase" time code before starting, and since I don't have to keep my computer running, my room is quieter—better for vocal recording. (The fan in my computer is *loud.* . . .)

Other uses for the output busses show up at mixdown time. If I've got four channels of backup vocals whose mix will stay constant, but whose overall volume is going to change, I assign them to a buss. If I need to adjust the volume of the backing vocals, I don't need to adjust all four faders—I can adjust the whole mix of backups with just one or two faders (one for mono, two for stereo). The output busses can also be used for additional effects sends in a pinch. If you've run out of effect sends and you need more, just connect an unused output buss to the input of the effect you need. You can then select this effect by switching the appropriate assignment switch on the channel you want effected.

There are a few extra switches in this section of the input module. The pan knob has a reverse switch, and it reserves the setting of the pan knob. The last two switches sit above the assignment switches. The first is a channel on/off switch, and it does just what the name implies. When switched off, no signal is passed through the channel—including the effects sends, although the insert points may still be active. The final switch is the "solo" switch, and it allows you to listen to just that channel, even when every other channel is playing. The solo function on this mixer is mono, prefader, post-eq, which, as you know, means that the eq settings can be heard when the solo switch is activated, while the fader settings have no effect. More advanced mixers have more capable solo functions, allowing you to select between "pfl" (prefader listen) and "solo in place," which is postfader and stereo. This way, you can hear the level of the soloed sound as well as the pan position. More than one solo button can be selected at a time, although this is most useful with a "solo in place" system.

The channel fader is the largest control on the input module, and it controls the final output level from the module. Generally, you shouldn't have to operate a fader much past the 0 dB point; if you find yourself doing this, recheck your trim setting for that channel. If you've used a very extreme cut in your eq settings, you may find that you have to boost the fader beyond the 0 dB point in order to compensate for what you've removed from the signal.

Now, here are some tricks involving the input module.

Use the Direct Outputs to Record

Here is the trick you can use most often: If your mixer has insert points (send/receive) or a direct output of at least one input module, you can connect the send or direct out of that channel and plug it directly into the input of your multitrack recorder. Let me show you an example. When recording acoustic guitar, I usually use my small diaphragm condenser mic, connect it into my last input module (channel 16 on my board), making sure that the phantom power is on. I then take a patch cable and connect it to the send portion of the insert points. The other end of the cable goes to the input on my multitrack. (I'm lucky — my mixer uses separate ¼" jacks for the inserts. Your mixer may use a different connector, such as an RCA jack, or if you aren't lucky, a ¼" stereo jack wired to send *and* receive. You'll have to hunt down the proper connector at Radio Shack.) If I'm using a compressor (which I usually am), I connect the send from the input to the input on the compressor, and the compressor output goes to the multitrack input. I set the trim control level as always, using the solo function and my ears; don't forget to set the trim without any eq! If I need to eq, it's no problem, since the sends are post-eq. I then record the track, the same way I would if I were using the output busses of the mixer. When it's time to record another track, say a double of the acoustic guitar, I just move the patch cable to the appropriate input on the multitrack.

When you use this scheme to record, be sure you know how to monitor the track you're recording: Listen through the tape machine, not through the input module the mic is plugged into. If you're recording with a stereo source, you can use two input modules. If you've previously been using the output busses to record, you'll notice increased clarity as well as reduced noise and distortion. Best of all, the improvement was free.

Cascading Tone Controls

In some extreme instances, one set of equalization controls is not enough. Maybe you need more than four bands, or you need extra boost at a certain frequency. In cases like these, you can use the send from the channel that needs the extra eq (let's say channel 1) and plug it into the LINE input of another channel (channel 2). Make the eq adjustments on channel 1 first, and listen *only* to channel 1. Once you've done the best you can, turn channel 1 off, so that it's no longer being heard. Now you can activate channel 2. (Be sure you've selected LINE as the source of channel 2.) You can now add any additional eq on channel 2, though the eq from channel 1 will still be active, since the insert send is post-eq and postfader. This trick uses up two channels, so I don't often use it, but it can save you when the basic channel eq isn't doing the job.

Parallel Channels

Sometimes I need drastic tone changes from one section of a mix to another on a particular channel—tape or MIDI instrument. In the heat of actually doing the mix, it can be very difficult to achieve the exact tone changes I want by turning several knobs to new positions; so, if I have an extra input on my mixer, I set up a "parallel channel," using a wiring scheme similar to the cascading tone-control setup. That is, I use the send from the channel that needs the help to the LINE in on the extra channel. I set one eq on the original channel, then I turn the eq off with the eq on/off switch. I turn the channel off, too; I'll be listening to the parallel from here on. Next, I turn on the parallel channel, and set up the separate eq. By simultaneously switching the two eq's, one to "on" and the other to "off," I get two very different settings that are completely repeatable. I have to be careful to make the switches when there's no signal present, so that the changes don't sound like a mistake.

Intentional Distortion

Have you ever heard Dave Edmund's version of "I Hear You Knockin' "? The lead vocal is incredibly distorted, and it sounds really cool. Maybe someday, someone else will have a huge hit with this effect. Here's how you can try it: Turn the trim knob on the mic channel all the way up. If you've got too much level, you can bring it down by sending it through an output buss and turning it down (remember, we *want* the distortion . . .) before sending the buss out to the multitrack.

Use Your Inserts

You already know how to use the send portion of a channel insert. Try hooking up individual effects to a channel insert. This will save you an effects send when you need only one channel processed. The most common processors are compressers and outboard eq's, but you can hook up chorus units, reverbs, multi-effects—whatever. If you're really feeling ambitious, you can try using guitar effects like wah-wah pedals, distortion units and various other stomp boxes. Be aware that line level (the signal strength of a channel insert) is much hotter than instrument level (the signal strength in a stomp box), so you may have to compensate by lowering the trim control. Also, some stomp boxes are more forgiving of too much level than others.

One very cool processor I use at the channel inserts is a MIDI controllable fader. This means I can use my sequencer to control the level of a channel with this device connected at insert. Since this unit has eight channels, I have eight channels of fader automation. There have been instances at mix time when I needed one syllable of the lead vocal turned up while the lead guitar needed to fade out while the stereo backup vocals gradually swelled. By using four channels of MIDI fader automation, I was able to "write" each move into my sequencer. When I was done, each move occurred flawlessly—time and time again.

I'm sure that your mixer has input modules that are different from mine. Perhaps your mixer has four or eight subs instead of sixteen, or maybe you don't have as many effects sends, although you may have more than me. You may also have a combination mixer/recorder—both pieces together in one box. The point is that most of the functions are similar from board to board, and once you get used to one, it's not too hard to work on another. With that in mind, let's move on to the next major section of a board, the submaster or buss module.

The Submaster Module

This submaster module is a little more involved than most. The first switch is the tape/monitor switch, and it is similar to the input selection switches on the input module. With the switch set to "monitor," this submaster module will "listen" to any input channels that are assigned, through the assignment switches, to it. For example, if this is submaster #4 and input channels #1 through #5 are assigned to "¾", anything on those tracks will come up at this submaster (providing that the pan knobs on the input channels aren't panned hard left—any channels panned hard left will only come up on submaster #3).

The next two controls, labeled "level" and "pan," work together to send whatever the fader is listening to over the master (left/right) stereo buss. These controls are postfader, so the fader must be turned up for these two knobs to work. Also, the submaster output (sometimes called "tape out," which you might have connected to your multitrack input—since this is submaster #4, you'd connect its output to multitrack input #4) is not affected by the level and pan knobs.

This mixer's submaster modules also have two effects sends that are switchable from pre to post, and a solo button. Some mixers have more involved subs that include additional functions, like eq. The final control is a fader, which is normally set to 0 dB, although in the illustration, I've left it set all the way down.

For some reason, submasters are confusing. In actual practice, they require little attention—you just set 'em and forget 'em. The way you set them depends on how you want to use them.

Using Submasters as Tape Sends

This is the most basic way to use your subs. You simply connect the "submaster out" of each sub to the appropriate inputs on your multitrack recorder (channel #1 out to tape in #1, etc.). Set your sub faders to 0 dB, and you're in business. Recording is simple. Assign the input channels you want to record with the assignment switches, select the same channel on your multitrack recorder, and

off you go. Once a tape track is recorded, you can listen through the input channel by selecting "tape" at the imput module; or, if you'd like, you can monitor the recorded track through the submaster by selecting "tape" with the submaster "tape/monitor" switch. Playing back the tape through the sub allows you to use the input module for other sounds—MIDI instruments, for example.

If your mixer has fewer subs than your multitrack recorder has inputs, you'll need to set up slightly differently. If you have four subs on your mixer and eight channels on your multitrack, hook up channels 1 through 4 normally. Many 8-track recorders automatically send inputs 1 through 4 to inputs 5 through 8. This means that to record on channel #7, you need to assign the input module(s) you want recorded to sub #3. Notice that if you set your multitrack to record on channels #3 and #7, the same thing will be recorded on both tracks. If your multitrack doesn't cascade the inputs (i.e., if each input is totally discrete), check to see if your mixer has more than one output jack for each sub out. You can then connect two input channels on your recorder to each sub out.

Using the Submaster as a Group

When I record lead vocals, I almost always record more than one performance, each on a separate track. At mix time, I may want to use parts of each performance at different points in the song. If I'm not in track trouble (i.e., I have enough tracks for everything), I'll assign all of the lead vocal tracks to a submaster, set the submaster to "monitor," and use the submaster fader to adjust the lead vocal volume during the mix. Since I use MIDI muting (I can turn input channels on and off with a MIDI note command), I can automate the job of selecting which vocal track is active, which means I only have to worry about operating the submaster fader. If you don't have MIDI muting, you'll have to turn the appropriate channels on and off manually—as long as there aren't too many tight switches to accomplish, you'll be fine.

The reason for using this arrangement is not obvious; after all, if you're already turning the input channels on and off, it's no big deal to operate the input channel faders. Why bother using the submaster at all? The reason is the submaster channel insert. At mix time, you'll probably want to use a compressor on the lead vocal. If you have three channels of lead vocal, you'll need three identical compressors. Even if you have three identical compressors, you can find a better use for them than tying them all to the lead vocal. By sending all three vocal tracks to a sub and using that sub's insert point to connect the compressor, you free up the two other compressors. If the sub has effects sends, you can use them instead of the input channel sends. The result will be a more consistent effects mix on the vocal.

This trick also works if you have only one lead-vocal track and a double; you'll find that the double blends in better when running through the same compressor.

Use the Submaster as an Additional Channel

If you have more instruments and tape tracks than input channels, you can use the sub as an additional channel. Let's say you need to plug in a drum machine. Simply connect the drum machine's output to the "return" portion of the submaster insert. (For stereo, use two subs.) Since you won't have the flexibility that an input module gives, plan on using the subs as channels for those instruments needing the least amount of tweaking. Many MIDI instruments have built-in effects and eq, so there's little reason to tie up an input channel—use the submaster instead. You can also use the subs as additional effects returns, providing that you're careful not to send the effect back into itself with the sub effects sends. By the way, since the "return" portion of the insert point is a nonadjustable line input, you'll probably need to run any MIDI instruments or effects wide open, volume up full.

If you have an extra mixer, you can connect MIDI instruments into it and return the output to a pair of submaster returns. This is a great way to expand the capability of a good sounding board that's short on inputs.

The Master Effects Section

The master effects section has two parts: send and return. The *sends* are simply master levels for each of the (in this case) six sends, and they control how much signal is sent out from the board to the particular effect. Normally, these knobs should be set at about 50 to 70 percent. On some mixers, there may be a "solo" switch at each send, which allows you to listen to what the send has assigned to it. The solo function also allows you to set the send levels more accurately, since the signal being soloed usually shows up on a meter.

The *return* section shown here is very similar to an input—the

AUXILLIARY RETURN

level

pan

AUXILLIARY SENDS

send 1   send 4   on/off

solo   solo   solo

                            L/R

send 2   send 5   1/2

solo   solo   3/4

                            5/6

send 3   send 6   7/8

solo   solo   9/10

                            11/12

                            13/14

                            15/16

signal from an effect is adjusted with the pan and level knobs and routed to the stereo buss or submasters. The on/off switch allows the effect return to be muted. (On this console, there are two stereo and two mono effects returns; yours will no doubt be different.)

Like the submasters, an effects return can be used as an input in a pinch. Since the returns are even more limited than the submasters, you may hardly ever use them this way, but you never know! I use one of my stereo effects returns as an input for a small mixer (eight inputs) that has three stereo effects returns and a CD player plugged into it. Instead of having only three stereo effects returning into my console, I have five (and don't forget that CD player . . .).

The Master Section

Just calling this "The Master Section" makes it sound important and complicated. It's not—once you've mastered (excuse the pun)

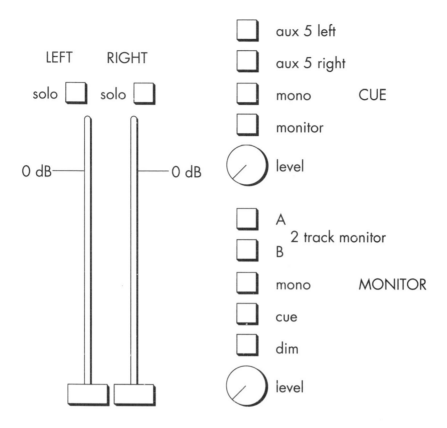

the rest of the board, the master section is cake. The main controls are the master faders, left and right (notice the "solo" switches). These faders control the level of the stereo (L/R) buss, which is connected to your mixdown machine of choice; DAT, 2-track analog or cassette. Normally, you set the master faders to 0 dB, and leave them there until the fade at mixdown. The master section also includes the "monitor" (or "control room") and "cue" (or "studio") controls. These subsections are very simple: the monitor section selects and controls the volume of what you will hear over your speakers, and the cue section does the same for the external head-phone system (if you have one).

On this particular mixer, the monitor switches select between the stereo buss (all switches up) and three other sources. These sources are "A" and "B," which are meant as mixdown recorder returns, and "cue" — whatever the cue section has selected. You can also make the monitors play whatever source is selected in mono.

Selecting mono will *not* make the stereo buss outputs mono; i.e., if you are doing a mix and you select "mono," your mix will still be stereo — you'll just be listening to it in mono. The "dim" switch lowers the level of the speakers by a healthy amount — helpful when the phone rings. Also, the dim switch does *not* affect the stereo buss output. The "level" control lets you set the speaker volume.

The cue switches select what the external headphone system will be listening to. In most home recording, the headphones can use the very same mix as the monitor, so you simply select "monitor" and set the volume with the level control. If you really need a headphone mix that is separate from the control room, you'll have to use the other cue sources — effects sends five and six. Try first using one of the sends (say, send five) and setting the cue to "mono." Any input channel with effects send five turned up will appear in the headphones. By selecting "aux 5 left" and "aux 6 right," you can have a separate stereo mix. Any input channels that need to appear in the headphones can be sent there by turning up effects sends five and six. You can control the pan by adjusting the relative levels of the two sends; more of send five means that sound will appear more to the left; more of send six will make the sound appear to be farther to the right. This is a very cumbersome procedure (read: a pain in the . . .), which is why I almost *never* make a separate mix for the headphones. If I'm working with someone who needs a different mix in order to sing, I change the mix to their liking. Whoever the performer is gets preference!

If your board has inserts on the master L/R outputs, you can use them for effects that will be used on an entire mix, such as stereo compression or stero eq. On my board, I use the master inserts for two channels of MIDI fader automation — all my fades are automated.

MULTITRACK RECORDERS

The multitrack machine is where you record parts that will ultimately be mixed into a finished product. Your multitrack is the heart of your studio — which is why nearly every studio is classified by its multitrack recorder. From 4-track analog cassette to 48-track digital, the multitrack machine defines the capabilities and limitations of the entire studio.

The basic concept and operation of all multitrack machines are more or less the same, so understanding one type of machine will get you started toward an understanding of all others. By the way, the type of machine is expressed in the number of tracks and the format (which is the type of tape or other medium used by the machine and any other characteristics that apply, such as tape speed and type of noise reduction, if any). For example, my machine is an analog 16-track ½" at 30 ips (inches per second) with Dolby C noise reduction. The differences between machines become significant when you take your tape to another studio: The slightest mismatch will make your tape incompatible with the other studio.

Analog Multitrack

Most multitrack machines are *analog* recorders, using the same basic technology as that developed in Germany during World War II. Put simply, analog machines take audio signals from microphones or other audio sources and turn them into electromagnetic pulses that are recorded onto magnetic tape. Tape quality, tape speed (faster is generally better), tape formulation, and track width (the actual width of the recorded section on tape) all have an effect on the sound quality of a particular machine.

The bottom-feeder format of analog multitrack is the cassette. The advantages of cassette are expense (low, for machine and tape), simplicity and convenience. The down side is poor performance. I find cassette multitracks barely listenable, but don't think I wouldn't use one if I had to. There are occasions when convenience, simplicity and expense are the overriding concerns.

Next up are the analog semipro open-reel machines. These range from ¼" 4- and 8-track machines to ½" 8- and 16-track machines to 1" 16- and 24-track machines (as well as a few other uncommon formats, such as the Akai 12-track, which uses its own special cassette). Tape speeds vary from 7.5 ips to 30 ips, and noise reduction is almost always used. Even the simplest of these machines vastly outperforms the cassette machines as far as sonic quality and flexibility are concerned. They also cost more, as does the tape. (Big surprise!)

The standard professional analog multitrack machine is the 24-track using 2" tape, running at either 15 or 30 ips. Noise reduction is an option with this format, either DBX or one of the Dolby types. Since these machines are quite expensive and large (about the size of a washing machine), they aren't commonly found in home studios. Pro machines also use much hotter signal levels, in and out of the machine, than semipro machines (+ 4 dB is the standard for pro machines, while -10 dB is the standard for semipro gear).

So much for analog machines. The other major types of multi-track recorders use digital audio rather than analog, and there are big differences between analog and digital.

Digital Multitrack

Until very recently, digital audio was a very expensive luxury, for pros only. Early 24-track digital machines sold for about $100,000, compared to about $30,000 for a top-of-the-line analog machine. Progress being what it is, the price of digital has plummeted, and today there are two semipro digital tape formats (Alesis ADAT and Tascam Hi-8) as well as several tapeless formats, many of which are nearly as affordable as analog. Let's look at the differences between analog and digital multitrack.

Digital recording, if it's done well, offers two primary advantages over analog recording — noise level and dynamic range. Digital recording should add no noise to what is being recorded, but analog recording adds quite a bit of noise. On analog tape, we hear the noise as hiss, and it's unavoidable. Most pro and semipro analog machines use noise reduction to minimize the hiss, but it's still there if you listen closely. (All noise reduction colors the signals somewhat — some types more than others.) Dynamic range refers to how loudly we can record without distortion and how quietly we can record without noise interfering. Dynamic range is expressed in dB (decibels). Analog tape has a dynamic range of about 65 dB; digital has a dynamic range closer to 90 dB or more. (This is one of those cases when bigger is better.) Digital wins on both accounts, so it must be better, right? Before we answer, let's consider some other factors.

First is resolution: How fine is the detail that the medium is capable of? Digital audio normally takes up to 48,000 (48k) "snapshots" per second per channel of sound and describes each "snapshot" as a sixteen-digit (bit) number in base 2. (It's important to realize that snapshots taken with a camera use various sizes of film; all other things being equal, the larger piece of film leads to higher resolution. The number of bits in digital recording is similar to the size of the piece of film in photography.) It is arguable that analog tape has a higher resolution than digital since it does not subdivide sound into "snapshots," but rather records more or less continuously. (Then again, how wide is a single magnetic particle on a piece of analog tape, and how much time does it record at a tape speed of 30 inches per second? . . . I'm even putting myself to sleep.)

A second factor is accuracy. Analog recording is inaccurate because of physical limitations of tape and magnetics, but the inaccuracies are small. Digital can have fewer inaccuracies, but there's a major problem; sound must be converted from analog to digital before it can be recorded. Why can't sound simply start out digitally? Simple — there are as yet no digital microphones (at least none I'm aware of). All microphones convert sound energy into electrical energy, which then must be converted to digital. The problem here is that more accurate analog-to-digital converters (A/D) "sound" better than others. As you might guess, better A/D converters generally cost more, up to thousands of dollars per channel. Bear in mind the amount of math being done, and it's easy to see why accuracy is important.

In actual use, the main differences between analog and digital are that digital is virtually noise-free and "colorless" — sounds recorded on digital don't change as they do in analog recording. The coloration caused by analog recording is often desirable, so before you jump into digital, you'll want to consider this factor. Also, digital audio must not be recorded too hot, or you'll get an "overload." Unlike analog tape, which gently distorts if you record too hot, digital audio is unforgiving. Any overloads will result in ugly, harsh distortion that cannot be corrected without re-recording.

Hard-Disk Recording

Normally, we record digital audio onto tape; when we turn the machine off, the tape has stored what we've recorded, and it's there waiting until we come back to record again. Barring flood, fire or thermonuclear blast (the electromagnetic radiation alone would erase every tape in town, along with the electronic ignition in every car), the tape is relatively safe for years. We can also record digital audio directly to a computer hard disk, bypassing tape entirely. We'll need about 5 megabytes of storage for each track minute of digital audio we want to record, which points out the main limitation of hard-disk recording — storage space. In most hard-disk recording systems, you can play or record no more than four tracks simultaneously, although you can record as many tracks as you want through overdubbing (you can have all the tracks you can store, but you can hear only four at a time). While the hard disk is a fine temporary storage medium, you should know that *all hard drives will fail.* A single power surge or a medium physical shock can wipe out *all* of your work. Additionally, one song may fill up your hard disk — what if you want to record another? For these reasons, hard-drive recordings must be backed up to another storage device, such as a DAT tape. One more problem: This takes time. If you have four five-minute tracks on your hard drive, it will take about ten minutes to store or load. If you have sixteen five-minute tracks, it will take forty minutes to store or load.

Hope you can find something to do while you are storing or loading, because your computer won't be available for anything else!

This storage bugaboo is the biggest drawback to hard-disk recording. Even storage to DAT is expensive in time and money. So why bother? The reason is that hard-disk recording systems offer unmatched flexibility in terms of editing and signal processing, in addition to having some other nifty features like unlimited virtual tracks.

First, let me explain hard-disk recording a little better. If you own a computer, you already have some idea what a hard drive does — it stores data, like a floppy drive, but with a much higher storage capacity and at a much greater speed. Remember that digital audio is nothing more than lots of 16-bit numbers in base 2 — data — and the connection should become clearer. Once audio is in the digital realm, it can be stored just like any other data — it just requries a lot of storage space. To store one minute of 16-bit digital audio at a sampling rate of 48,000 (snapshots) per second requires about 5 meg of storage capacity (1 meg = 1 million bits). This is for mono only; if you want stereo, double the 5 meg figure to 10 meg. If you want four tracks, double this figure again to 20 meg. Get the idea? If you wanted to store a stereo mix of a three-minute song on floppies, you'd need about twenty high-density floppies! Besides being cumbersome, the time it takes for the computer to read or write the disks would make this prospect impossible. With a 100-meg hard drive (a bare minimum that will frustrate you and that you will quickly outgrow), however, access time is greatly reduced and storage is greatly increased. We can store about ten minutes of 16-bit stereo audio on a drive this big.

So, now we have a hard drive. Next, we need a computer, preferably a fast one. The computer should have its own hard drive, separate from our "big" 100 meg, to store the computer's operating system, any software you'll be using, and any storage you'll need related to these functions. The 100-meg drive is to be used only for digital audio. To get the computer and the digital audio drive to talk to each other, you'll need a special adapter card that fits into your computer and some specialized software that coordinates the whole thing. On the adapter card may be some *d/a* (digital to analog) converters, or you may need to get stand-alone d/a converters. There should also be some capability for backing up the digital audio, probably to DAT. You should be able to use your own DAT machine, providing it will record at the same sampling rates as the hard-disk recorder. If your DAT machine records only at 48k, be sure that you don't do any work on the hard disk recorder at 44k.

The first use you might have for your new hard-disk recorder could be to edit some existing mixes you have. Suppose you have a song with two verses before the first chorus, and you want to take out the second verse. On DAT, you simply can't edit. All you do is record your mix into the hard drive, skipping the d/a converters and going directly into the digital inputs. The computer will write in a continuous fashion to the hard drive; in other words, the hard drive will be working the whole time you are recording. When you finish recording, you will be able to play the mix from the computer and start at any location. "Rewind" time will be very brief, compared to a tape recorder. The computer will display what the sound "looks" like, along with time indications showing where you are in the song. Once you locate the point where the edit is to begin, you mark it, and locate the point where the edit is to stop. Mark this point, instruct the computer to play the mix without the area you've marked, and listen to make sure the edit sounds OK.

Here's where the fun starts. The edit points probably don't sound OK—you might hear a click, or the timing feels wrong—so you'll have to do some fine-tuning. Try sliding the edit point earlier or later until the timing feels right. Since all you are changing is a marker, this type of editing is *nondestructive*. The mix itself has not changed; remove the markers and the missing verse reappears. If there is a click or a sonic mismatch at the edit point, you can try a *crossfade*. This is basically a blending of the sounds at the edit point over a very short period of time; it can smooth out rough transitions.

Other editing functions include changing the tempo of the song without affecting the pitch, changing the pitch without affecting the tempo, compression and reverse play. Imagine the hours you could waste playing around with this toy! Once you're done, just play the edited mix and record it back into your DAT machine. Be sure to skip the DAT machine's a/d converters and go digital in, and don't erase your original DAT mix. Working like this, you won't even need to back up your hard drive: the remix is already stored on DAT.

So far, we're talking only stereo. Let's get serious, and go for a 4-track hard-disk recorder. Our 100-meg drive will still work, although it will allow only five minutes of continuous 4-track recording time. The big difference in our system will be the interface card and the software, which have been changed to accommodate 4-track audio. As long as we record no more than two tracks at once, we can get by with only two d/a converters.

You can overdub as many times as you want (these are called *virtual tracks*), although you can hear only four tracks at any one time. This means that you can even have five tracks playing, as long as no more than four play simultaneously. If that doesn't give you enough flexibility, you can also mix four tracks together into one new track, and then keep recording. The main limitation is (again) hard-disk space. When you mix tracks, you won't be adding any noise or lose any generations because you'll mix in the computer — entirely in the digital realm (great name for a band . . .). You'll also be able to use built-in DSP (digital sound processing) functions, like compression, echo, flange and pitch change. Be aware, though, that any mixing is destructive — you won't be able to unmix unless you've kept the original tracks.

Other cool uses of a 4-track hard-disk recorder include recording lots of vocal takes, and combining (comping) them onto one track. Pitch and timing problems can be isolated and corrected (within limits), and level differences (too loud, too soft) can be evened out.

The danger of having all of this editing power is, of course, overusing it — spending more time editing than recording or writing. Do enough editing and you can boil the passion out of anything — you also could find yourself doing nothing but t*rd polishing. It might be fun, but it's t*rd polishing nonetheless. It's much more fun polishing diamonds!

(I have one caveat to those considering moving to digital recording: Be sure that the machine you want to buy will do what it says *before* you buy it. I have a friend who spent a large sum of money on a hard-disk system, only to find out the software was buggy.

He'll be waiting for a few months for the software update. Another friend is having problems with his tape-based digital multitrack; it won't always go into *record* when he wants it to—another software bug. So be bold, with caution!)

MICROPHONES

There are only two types of microphones you'll need to know about for most recording: the *dynamic* and the *condenser*. The most obvious difference between the two is that condenser mics require phantom power (usually 24 or 48 volts) or a battery to function. Dynamic mics will work as soon as you plug them in. Confused? Let me explain.

Remember the science experiments on electricity we all did in grade school, the ones with the magnet, the coil of wire and the light bulb? As you recall (in the dim corridors of your memory, if you were paying as much attention as I was back then), you can create electricity by moving the magnet within the coil or moving the coil around the magnet. The electricity you made would light the bulb. (This never fails to impress second-grade boys.)

A dynamic mic works on these principles. The mic has a diaphragm, which is connected to a coil, which fits in a gap cut into a magnet. When sound is created, vibrations travel through the air, hitting the diaphragm, which responds by moving. Since the coil is connected to the diaphragm, it moves, too, and since the coil is sitting inside a magnet, electricity is produced. Even though it's a very small amount of electricity, it's enough to be amplified and sent to a tape recorder and mixed and signed to a label and released— and to create a big hit.

A condenser mic also has a diaphragm, but the diaphragm needs to be charged with a small amount of current (from a battery or phantom power supply—which may be built into your mixer, or can be bought as a separate box) in order to work. Since the diaphragm doesn't need to drive a heavy coil of wire, condenser mics are much more sensitive than dynamic mics; however, they can also be easier to overdrive and distort. (This high sensitivity makes most condenser mics less-than-ideal choices for very loud sounds, such as drums or screamingly loud rock guitar. In these cases, a good dynamic will do a much better job.) Condenser mics also require much more careful handling than dynamics—just dropping a condenser mic could cost you hundreds of dollars to rebuild. Yes, condenser mics are usually more expensive then dynamics.

Both dynamic and condenser mics are also categorized by the size of their diaphragms—large or small. One way to understand how diaphragm size makes a difference is to compare microphones to speakers and diaphragm size to speaker size. Large speakers handle low frequencies better, and small speakers handle high frequencies better. Small diaphragm mics are better for sounds with lots of high-frequency content (like acoustic guitars and small percussion); large diaphragm mics work better when you need to capture warmer sounds, although this shouldn't keep you from trying using a large diaphragm mic to record a finger cymbal.

Use the Best Microphone You Can Get

If you are a singer, a guitarist, a sax player, or if you own your own studio, you need to use a great mic. If you can't afford to buy one, or if you don't know which mic is best for your purposes, rent one from a studio rental service. To start, I'd suggest a large diaphragm condenser mic, like an AKG-414 or a Neumann TLM-170. Both these mics are expensive, as much as a good multitimbral MIDI keyboard, but the mic will be a better investment; just look at the prices of used MIDI gear compared with used mic prices. You'll find that high-quality mics hold their value for much longer. Consider the mic a lifetime investment.

Get a Pop Filter

Condenser mics are very sensitive—that's why they are so good for vocals—but they are so sensitive that a normally articulated *p* can cause a very nasty *pop* sound. You should therefore *always* use a pop filter. You can buy one, or if you are cheap (like me), you can build one. First, get some nylon stockings or pantyhose. (Have some class and spring for the new ones.) Next, take a wire clotheshanger apart and rebend the wire into a circle about 8″ across. Leave the excess wire, so that the hanger now looks like a balloon with a string. Put one of the stockings over the balloon part, cut away the excess stocking, and connect the extra wire to the top of your mic stand. (I use duct tape.) Now all you need to do is position the flat surface of the stocking between the singer and the diaphragm of the mic. I usually set mine about 2″ or 3″ from the diaphragm and let the singer sing a similar distance from the nylon. Some singers like to sing with their lips actually touching the nylon. (Don't get me started. . . .) In this case, move the filter farther from the mic.

How Close?

Close miking (less than 12″ from the diaphragm) is the mainstay of home recording for mostly one reason—noise. You won't hear your neighbor's plumbing through the vocal track if you mic closely, but be careful! Getting the mic too close will result in an excessively heavy tone. *How* close will vary from mic to mic, so you'll just have to use your ears. For example, if you are working with a singer, have him or her move in and out in relation to the mic while you listen. Too far back and you'll hear the trucks driving by out in the street. Too close, and the singer will sound fifty pounds heavier.

As you get more experienced with mics, you'll notice the sonic differences between close and distant miking, such as ambience. The further away the mic, the more ambient sound you'll pick up. Sometimes this is desirable; use your artistic discretion. There's an old recording axiom: Distance equals depth. Listen to a good recording of a symphony and notice the front-to-back feeling of the sound. You can use this in your demos by varying the miking distances of various instruments. Experiment and listen.

Look for the Sweet Spot(s)

When setting up a mic, take the time to listen to the sound you want to record. Listen with your ears. As you listen, move around, looking for the place the sound sounds best; that's a good place to start. If you have someone to assist you, listen over speakers or headphones, and have the musician play while your assistant moves the mic around. Notice how much the sound changes. There will be a definite mic placement where the instrument sounds much better than other placements. (This technique works great for acoustic instruments.) When I'm looking for sweet spots, I listen for the sound over the mic to "lock in." Once you get sensitized to listening for sweet spots, they almost jump out at you.

Very often, the mic will need to be placed at an angle (off-axis) to the sound you want to record. For example, when miking an acoustic guitar, the natural tendency is to aim the mic straight into the soundhole. For myself, I have found that angling the mic at about 45 degrees to the soundhole works well. If the sound is too boomy, I simply change the point the mic is aiming at by a few inches toward the fingerboard.

Vocalists need to be careful with their aim. The tendency is for singers to move around as they get into a performance, resulting in inconsistent sound. If you can get your singers to find and hold a sweet spot, the vocal track will be much more sonically tight.

Use Mic Technique Instead of EQ

The less eq you use, the better. Why? Eq always adds noise and distortion, even when you are using high-quality equalizers. Very often, you can get the desired timbre without eq. Here's how:

First, get the instrument you are recording sounding as good as possible. (If you are miking a guitar amp, get the amp to sound just the way you want.) When you listen to the sound, listen at the same angle as you will be miking, and get as close to the sound as you can stand — don't hurt your ears. Once you are satisfied, position the mic where your ears were, pointing toward the sound. Listen over headphones or speakers for the sweet spot (see above). If the tone is not quite what you want, change the angle of the mic, as if the sound source were the earth and the mic were the moon. Keep the mic aimed at the center of the sound source, and listen to the differences as you change orbit. Once you've found the best-sounding spot, try rotating the mic on its own axis without changing the mic location in relation to the sound. You should again hear drastic tone changes. Use your ears and choose the sound you like best. If you have more than one mic to choose from, repeat this procedure with each mic until you find the one that works best. Once you've done this several times, you'll have a pretty good idea which mic to reach for in each situation. (It's just like golf: "I think I'll use my 3 iron. . . .")

Just as each sound will have a sweet spot, you will find that each sound also has ugly spots — places where the sound is harsh, or mixed with unwanted noise (breath sounds, string noise, etc.). Avoid these unless you like them.

If you take the time to "tune" the mic like this, you'll be able to use little or no eq.

Using Multipattern Mics

Many high-quality recording mics have a switch to adjust the pickup pattern of the mic. The range may be something like this: *cardiod* (picks up sound from the front of the mic only and rejects sound from the rear), *omnidirectional* (picks up sound on all sides —

not the top or bottom—in a 360 degree pattern), and *figure-eight* (picks up sound in the front and rear of the mic and rejects the sides). Normally for home recording, you'll want to use the cardiod pattern, since this pattern rejects sounds (such as street and neighbor noises) not in front of the mic. Sometimes the figure-eight pattern is useful, such as with two singers or guitarists facing each other, but even in these cases, I end up having both singers facing into the cardiod pattern—it just sounds punchier to me. Both singers need to be extra careful with their aim when singing into a cardiod pattern. It's also nice if they've both brushed their teeth—nothing worse than having to sing next to someone with birdcage breath.

If you have a very quiet and dead room to record in, try the omnidirectional setting—the sound will be great, but you'll have no noise rejection. Also, some mics have a *hyper-cardiod* setting—just like the cardiod, only tighter. Interestingly, the hyper-cardiod allows you to use the mic at a greater distance from the sound source while maintaining a high degree of rejection outside the pattern. In other words, when you use the hyper-cardiod, try backing away from it.

Set the Mic Preamp Gain Properly

The first control at the top of an input channel is usually the preamp gain. This the first stage of amplification for the mic signal, and you can blow the whole deal by setting the gain too high or too low.

I'll show you what I mean. Plug in a mic, and listen to it on headphones. Adjust the gain control all the way up, turn the headphone level down to a comfortable level, and speak loudly into the mic. You should be hearing a very distorted sound, unless you have set an attenuator (on the imput channel or the mic itself) too low. If your mixer has individual channel peak displays (usually a red LED), you should be seeing some indication of the distortion; the red light comes on.

Now try turning the gain control all the way down. You'll need to turn the headphones up to compensate for the loss of gain in the first stage. When you listen now, you probably won't hear any distortion, but you will hear an increase in *circuit* noise, usually hiss or hum (as opposed to *ambient* noise, or noise in the room). Somewhere between distortion (gain set too high) and noise (gain set too low) is the ideal gain setting for the particular preamp, microphone and sound source. Lots of experimentation is necessary in order to train your ears to know what to listen for; that's why it's a good idea to try setting the gain too high or too low, so you can hear the distortion or noise you'll be getting. Once again, you might like the sound of distortion.

When recording a very loud sound, you may need to use attenuation to get the gain control low enough to avoid distortion. Look for a switch near the preamp gain, perhaps labeled *10* or *20*; engaging this switch will lower the gain level by an additional 10 or 20 dB. You should now be able to adjust the preamp gain level to accommodate the sound you are working with. If you are still getting distortion, the mic itself may be overloading. You now have three choices: Either make the sound quieter, move the mic away from the sound, or engage the attenuator on the mic (if it has one). Sometimes, the attenuator for the mic is inside the mic; it might be in the battery compartment, for example.

Make a Vocal Corner

When you are recording with a microphone, you're not just recording a sound source — you're also recording reflected sounds. These are the sounds that have bounced off the walls in your room, and they will color the sounds you want to record. If you like the sounds your room adds, great. If you don't, or if you don't want this particular room sound on everything you record, you can make a dead section of the room, which will minimize the reflected sounds. The cheapest way to do this is to hang an old blanket on the wall. If you fold the blanket in two and hang it in a corner, you'll have the beginnings of a vocal corner. Try recording with the singer facing into the vocal corner first (although my studio is so small that I have singers sing facing out of the corner). Be sure that there are no walls behind the singer that are parallel to the microphone diaphragm, since parallel surfaces will reflect the most sound back into the mic.

To improve your vocal corner for just a little bit of money, you can buy sound-deadening foam to use instead of blankets. The stuff I use is 2″ thick and has an egg-carton pattern on it; it was also very cheap. More expensive foam will last longer and look better.

COMPRESSION

The idea of compression is simple: reducing the dynamic range of sound. What is *dynamic range*? Simply, it is the distance between the loudest and softest level of a sound. Think of a trumpet player playing a solo. The piece may start out quietly, so quiet that the audience may have to strain to hear it, then suddenly become quite loud. If you were to record this performance, you would need to have some control over the dynamic range to enable the quiet parts to be heard and to keep the loud parts from being overbearing.

Dynamic range is also used to express the dynamic capability of audio equipment and recording/broadcasting media. In this case, the dynamic range is the distance between the noise floor and the level where distortion occurs. When a signal that is to be recorded exceeds the dynamic range of a recording medium, such as analog tape, then the dynamic range of the incoming signal must be reduced in order to avoid distortion on the loudest parts and the intrusion of noise on the quietest parts.

The most basic way of reducing dynamic range is called *gain riding*. The engineer simply adjusts by hand the level of the sound being recorded, turning it down when things get too loud and cranking it when sounds are too quiet. This technique works well, depending on the engineer and the predictability of the sound source. With an unpredictable source, the job becomes impossible.

Compressors were designed to take the place of gain riding, automatically adjusting the level of a sound by varying degrees. The basic concept is simple: For each dB put into the compressor, the compressor puts out a fraction of a dB. You (the user) get to set the ratio between input and output. For example, a compression ratio of 3:1 means that for every 3 dB at input, there will be only 1 dB at output. It was soon realized that the compressor could do more than simple gain riding—extreme sonic modifications were now possible.

There are usually additional settings to adjust. The *threshold* control lets you choose at which point the compressor begins to work. It can be set so that the compressor is always working (threshold set very low: All levels are louder than threshold), or it can be set to compress only louder sounds (threshold set higher: Compression occurs only when sound level exceeds threshold). If the threshold is set so high that no sound levels exceed the threshold, there will be no compression.

Some compressors have "attack" and "release" controls. These let you set how quickly the compressor acts once the threshold has been crossed, and how long the compression setting is held. Once the compression is released, it will be off until the threshold is crossed again. With a slow attack setting, sounds that exceed the threshold will pass uncompressed until the attack time has been reached.

Other common controls on compressors allow you to set input and/or output levels; choose between normal compression and "soft-knee" compression; select various metering modes; and allow the linking of two identical compressors for stereo mode.

The difference between normal compression and soft-knee (or "over easy") is important. During normal compression, crossing the threshold results in an immediate transition from no compression to whatever compression ratio you've selected. During soft-knee compression, the transition is gradual, and the result is that soft-knee compression is generally less obvious to the ear. Vocals can be compressed without sounding compressed.

"There's Only One Way to Use a Compressor"
Yeah, right. You must experiment with your compressor—it's a powerful tool that can be used in many different ways in many different situations. Get creative: Compress the send to your reverb—compress the reverb return! Go wild and make up your own sounds.

"All Compressors Sound the Same"
Wrong again. Each compressor sounds very different. Some will be better for one job; others will sound better for other jobs. You'll have to do lots of experimenting to see what works best for you. It's OK if you've got only one compressor; you'll get really good with it! Then, when you can afford another, you'll have a good idea of what you need next.

Compare, Compare, Compare!
Be sure to compare the sound you are working on in its compressed and uncompressed versions, especially if you are using a compressor that you aren't completely familiar with. If the compressor doesn't improve the sound or help you fit an extreme dynamic range onto tape, don't use it!

Setting the Threshold and Ratio
By far, the most critical adjustments are the threshold and ratio controls. Since they interact somewhat, it can be difficult to adjust

them confidently. One approach is an engineering approach: "I look at the meters and see how far over *0 dB* the signal goes, and I calculate. . . ." My preference is to approach the compressor as if it were an extension of the instrument or voice I want to compress, and make adjustments by feel. This doesn't mean that I ignore standard engineering practices; I'm careful to set input and output levels properly and to follow similar procedures.

Start with the threshold very high (all the way up) and the compression ratio set low; 2:1 or 3:1 will be fine. As you listen to the sound you want to compress, bring the threshold level down until the threshold indicator begins to flash. At this point, you should start to hear compression occurring. If you continue lowering the threshold, more and more of the sound will be getting compressed, until the entire signal is compressed. Notice that the sound level drops as the threshold is lowered. Return the threshold setting to the point where the threshold indicator is flashing on and off, indicating that some of the signal is being compressed and some is not. Now, adjust the ratio control. Start by setting the ratio to its lowest setting, 1:1. At this setting there will be no compression, regardless of the threshold control's setting. Adjust the ratio up, and listen. If you can, set your compressor's meter to read "gain change." This will give you a visual indication as to how much the signal is being turned down by the compressor. Notice that the gain change increases as the ratio increases, and that the sound level drops a bit as the ratio control is set higher and higher.

I hope you now understand how these two controls interact. Developing expertise with the compressor requires that you experiment with various sounds and settings—the compressor is not a simple, on/off device. If you're a guitarist, you can feel the differences in various compressor settings—the one that feels best to you will often inspire a better performance.

Compress in Stages

Since compression is an irreversible process, it's a good idea to compress in stages, a little at tracking and a little at mixdown. The compression will be more subtle and controllable, and you won't have that all-too-common problem of too much compression. If you have only one compressor, you'll be able to use this scheme on only one sound, probably the lead vocal. This will work fine, even if you need to compress the guitars and bass, etc. An overcompressed bass is less of a sonic problem than an overcompressed vocal.

Compressing a Vocal

Depending on the singer, you can use a compressor to smooth out levels and avoid an oversaturated tape. If the singer is very experienced, you may not need much compression — good mic technique can make all the difference. Use a low-compression ratio and a high threshold, so that only the loudest notes will be caught by the compressor. The low ratio will soften the peaks slightly. I almost always use soft-knee compression for vocals.

With other singers, you'll need to use more compression — higher ratios and lower thresholds. Be careful: As compression increases, electronic noise (hiss and hum) and noise problems within the room increase. You'll also notice that any vocal problems such as loud breathing and other mouth noises, will be accentuated. Your job is to find the proper amount of compression for each situation.

Limiting

Limiting differs from compression. The idea is that a limiter will not allow a signal to get any louder than the threshold setting. Think of limiting as a ceiling beyond which no sound may pass. Limiting is useful for squashing exteme transients — drums, for example.

Ganged Compressors

If you've got two compressors, you can connect them in series, the output of one into the input of another. The first compressor is set with a high threshold and a high compression ratio, while the second is set for light to medium compression and a moderate threshold. The first compressor stops any extreme peaks; it's essentially a limiter. The second compressor smooths out the signal. This trick works with instruments that have a very expressive dynamic capability, such as brass instruments. I've used this setup on sax solos; the performer would play softly and intimately, then suddenly blast out. The limiting compressor stopped the blast from distorting the tape, and the second compressor provided the smoothness we needed. Since the limiter was first in the chain, the second compressor never "saw" the blasts.

Level Smoothing

Some instruments almost demand compression in order to sound good. Electric bass is one example. Without compression, even great players have trouble maintaining a steady level, and unless the instrument is outstanding, it can be difficult getting the sound to sustain. Compressing the bass lets you even out all the loud bits and causes the sustained notes to appear louder. (I should point out that if you are using an amplifier and speaker that is then being miked to record bass, you can often do very well without compression. The amp and speaker will compress the bass on their own.) As always, start with a great sound before you start to compress. Once you've achieved the best sound you can, begin compressing with moderate (3:1, 4:1) compression ratios and with the threshold set low enough that nearly every note is caught by the compressor. If the part is very percussive or punchy, you'll want to experiment with normal (hard-knee) compression, which often adds to the punchiness. If the part is smooth, try the soft-knee setting, which will be more subtle.

Stereo Compression

To compress a stereo source, you'll need a stereo compressor or two identical compressors that can be "linked" for stereo. First, be sure that the source you want to compress is really stereo: If all you need to do is to compress two tracks of layered backing vocals (both tracks are mono), you can use two different compressors in a pinch, or two identical compressors that haven't been linked. If your track to be compressed is stereo, then linking is a must in order to avoid left-to-right balancing changes and stereo-imaging problems.

If your intention is to compress a full mix, you might want to consider doing a normal, uncompressed mix to DAT first. If you can borrow another DAT machine, you can play back this mix into the stereo compressor and record the new, compressed version on the second DAT. By doing this job this way, you'll keep your compressors free for other jobs at mixdown, and you'll be able to change the amount of compression later if you change your mind. If you insist on compressing at mixdown, you'll need to do a full remix if you want to change anything. I have found that remixes never sound the same as the original mix. They may sound better or worse, but not the same.

Except for these concerns, stereo compression is the same as mono compression. Trust your ears.

De-essing With a Compressor

Every once in a while, you may run into a situation involving a vocal track with very heavy sibilance—*s*'s. Sometimes it's a singer who stresses *s*'s (oh no, a rhyme . . .), and sometimes it's a case of using the wrong microphone or eq for the singer. At mix time, there's trouble: all you hear are the *s*'s, and they distract from the track.

What you need is a de-esser. Unfortunately, you don't have one. However, if you have a compressor and an equalizer (a 10-band graphic or a parametric), you might be able to hook them up into a real live de-esser. The critical component is your compressor. You'll need to find out if yours has a "detector" input or a "side chain" loop. Look on the back panel. If you have a side chain loop, simply hook the equalizer in, sending from the loop to the eq and from the eq back to the loop. You then run the track to be de-essed into the compressor.

If your compressor has a detector input, you'll have to do a little more work. First, you'll have to split the signal from the track you want to de-ess with a "y" adapter or a "mult" on your patch bay. One side of the split goes to the regular compressor input, while the other goes to the eq input. The eq output goes to the detector input. On my compressor, the normal input and the detector input are on a barrier strip, and connections are made with screws. If your compressor is set up this way, you'll notice that there is a metal strap that connects the normal input to the detector input, so that anything connected to the normal in is also connected to the detector in. The reason for this is that most often we want the compressor to make its "decisions" on when to compress based on what the signal being sent into it is doing; as the signal gets louder, it crosses the threshold and compression begins. What we want to do now is to have the compressor decide to work based on the signal coming from the eq only, so you must remove the metal strap that connects the detector in and the normal in. Don't lose it—you'll need to replace it when the de-essing job is over. If your compressor doesn't use the barrier strip method, it will most likely have a switch that selects between normal operation and separate detector or side chain operation. If you can, consult the manual to make sure you've got everything hooked up properly.

Once you've figured out all the connections for your system, you'll be ready to start. The idea here is that we want to make the compressor very sensitive to the *s*'s and to leave everything else alone. To do this, we simply boost the frequency we want to compress—in this case, around 2 kHz. If you've got a parametric, you can really dial in the band you want to effect, although the graphic will also work well. Boost the selected frequency to the max. This boosted signal will be telling the detector, "Whenever you hear this, compress." You'll now need to adjust the compressor. Start with a high compression ratio—10:1 or more—and adjust the threshold down until the vocal track is getting compressed, hopefully only on the *s*'s. You will most likely need to do a bit of fine-tuning in order to get the effect you want, so experiment away. If you have problems hooking this up and getting it to work, have no fear. It took me several hours and a few phone calls to get mine to work the first time. If necessary, call the compressor manufacturer and ask for customer support. They'll be able to help with your specific compressor.

EQUALIZATION

The primary sound-shaping tools you have in your studio (after level-setting controls) are the equalizers. There are many different types of equalizers; some are better suited for certain jobs than others, so it's important to know how to approach each type.

First, some basics. Sound is vibration. The speed of the vibration is called *frequency*, which is expressed in Hz (Hertz); for example, a sound that has a frequency of 20 cycles per second is written as *20 Hz*. The lowest sound a normal human being can hear is 20 Hz, and the highest sound a normal human being can hear is 20,000 Hz, which is usually written as 10 kHz (kilohertz).

If you raise the pitch of a sound by one octave, you have doubled the frequency. Concert *A* is usually 440 Hz (although there are occasions when concert *A* varies; some symphonies use 338 Hz, and others use 441 Hz). *A* above concert *A* is 880 Hz—double the frequency again, and you get 1,720—*A* the next octave up. All of this means that the interval from 20 Hz to 40 Hz is the same as the interval from 10 kHz to 20 kHz: one octave.

The speed of the vibration is the frequency, and the depth of the vibration is the *amplitude*, which is expressed in dB (decibels). If you can visualize a diving board that has just been used, you'll understand the relationship between frequency and amplitude. After the diver leaves the board, the board continues to move up and down.

The distance the board travels up and down is the amplitude; the speed at which it moves up and down is the frequency. Notice that the frequency of the board will stay more or less the same as the amplitude decreases—in other words, the sound of the board does not change pitch as its volume decreases. Even after the sound of the board is inaudible, you can feel vibration by putting your hand on the board. Strings on a guitar are very similar to the diving board: when you pluck a string, it vibrates at one pitch. The sound is loudest when it is first plucked, and the string travels back and forth the farthest at this time. As the amplitude decreases, the pitch of the string stays the same.

When a sound doubles in amplitude, the increase is 3 dB. Interestingly, our ears don't respond to amplitude changes the way you might expect; a 3 dB increase is not heard as twice as loud. To double the apparent volume of a sound, it is necessary to increase amplitude by 10 dB, which is like multiplying by ten! To go from 70 dB to 80 dB means that apparent volume has doubled, while amplitude has increased tenfold.

When you work with an equalizer, you will be cutting or boosting frequencies expressed in Hz by levels expressed in dB.

OK, you can wake up now. You don't need to understand all this at once, but you may have questions later that this brief section could clear up. Let's move on to the actual equalizers.

Types of Equalizers

The simplest equalizers in normal studio use are the standard "bass/treble" controls, just like those found on your stereo system. You can think of each control as a volume control for a portion of the sound. The bass control is like a volume control for low frequencies only (usually from 100 Hz down); the treble control covers high frequencies only (from about 5 kHz up). This type of eq controls a wide range of frequencies, so you can consider it a "wide brush." You should also notice that this type of eq is normally a "shelving" type—if the eq says it is boosting 3 dB at 5 kHz, that 3 dB boost applies to *all* frequencies above 5 kHz.

The next type of eq includes one or more controls for the middle-frequency ranges, from 100 Hz to 5 kHz or so. The middle control is normally not a shelving control; instead, a peak/dip control is used, since a shelving control would affect all frequencies above or below the center frequency. The shelving control allows you to ad-

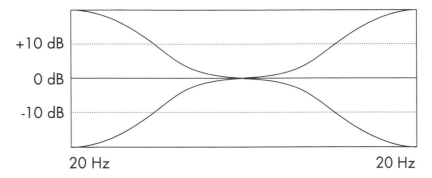

Shelving eq

just the frequencies around the center frequency only, leaving the other ranges unaffected. If an equalizer allows you to shift the center frequency, it is called a *quasi-parametric* eq. This feature lets you find the specific frequency you wish to adjust; it's very helpful. The next level of equalizer is the *parametric* eq, which not only lets you select the frequency you want to adjust, it also lets you set the width of the peak or dip. This type of equalizer can be set to boost or cut a very narrow and specific frequency range as well as a very broad and specific frequency range. The width of the eq is expressed as q. You won't need to use this measurement very often, but sometimes q is the label for the width control. A low q number is wider than a high q.

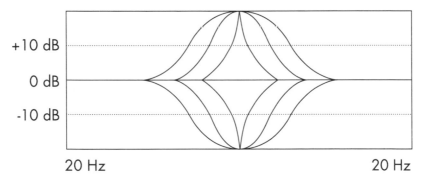

Parametric eq

Another major type of equalizer is the *graphic* eq. In a graphic eq, the full range of frequencies is broken into equal sections, and each section has a sliding fader control. Each fader is a peak/dip type, and the "off" setting is in the middle of the fader's throw—neither boosting nor cutting. The standard graphic is a 10-band, with ten controls, each of which covers about one octave of human hearing.

There is yet another category of equalizer, and for lack of a better word I'll call them *enhancers*. Enhancers do more than eq; one type adds minute amounts of delay at certain frequencies (which is supposed to correct frequency-based timing misalignments caused by speakers), as well as making automatic eq adjustments based on the signal you're feeding it. Other enhancers do entirely different tricks, such as adding an "emphasis" at a frequency you select, which is blended into the original signal. These tools have become standards, even in very basic studios, since they provide a huge amount of sonic manipulation at a very low cost. Describing what they sound like is difficult, although I use mine to add "sparkle" to individual tracks and "sheen" to my mixes. These devices are nearly the magical makes-anything-sound-better box, but they are also easy to overuse, to the point that they become a makes-anything-sound-thin-and-annoying box.

Don't Overdo It

Hey, look. Using eq is fun. You can make profound sonic changes with just a few simple controls, and besides, if you weren't supposed to use eq, why did your mixer come with eq on *every* channel? You're not getting your money's worth if you don't use every knob.

Think again, Resistor-head. Even putting an eq that is set flat (all controls centered—no eq) into a circuit adds noise and distortion to a sound. You probably won't hear it if you use a very expensive eq, but on any eq you're likely to find in a home studio, the problem may be all too audible. When you start boosting the eq, you'll only make things worse, since any noise inherent in the signal will be boosted right along with the program material. This doesn't mean you should never use your eq; it means you should try some other approaches before you go stampeding after the equalizers.

Leave Unused EQ Switched Out

This tip applies to mixers that have an eq switch on each input channel: If you aren't using the eq, switch it out, rather than setting the eq flat. The result: less noise and distortion.

Start With Great Sounds

It's best to get the instrument you're recording sounding right first, before trying to "fix" it with the eq. If the acoustic guitar is too dull, change strings. If it's too boomy, tape a piece of shirt cardboard over the soundhole. (Use removable tape for best results.) Have the guitarist try a variety of different picks—they make a huge difference in how the guitar sounds. For electric guitar, change guitars, amps, speakers—whatever works. Have the drummer carefully tune his drums before you worry about how to make them sound better. The point is to spend the time working on the sound first.

Use Your Best-Sounding Room

Even if your studio is in a small apartment, you can increase your sonic options by locating the instrument you're recording in flattering surroundings. Try miking a singer in your bathroom, your living room, your kitchen. You'll be shocked at how much difference each makes.

Use Mic Technique Instead of EQ

When miking an instrument, start with the eq flat. Take the time to move the microphone around a bit to find a sweet spot. Next, try changing the angle of the microphone in relation to the sound; this will change the timbre of the instrument quite a bit. If you still feel like reaching for the eq, try another microphone and repeat the above procedures.

Remember that a guitar speaker usually sounds brighter toward the center, near the voice coil, so adjust mic placement accordingly.

Edit Keyboard Sounds

If you use electronic keyboards (MIDI or otherwise) you can often edit the sounds to get what you want. The most obvious fix is for the synth that's not bright enough; simply open up the filter. (Some synths have their own effects and eq built in. Depending on how the eq is designed, it may work better and easier than the eq on your mixer.

Even after all this, there are times when eq is the only answer. If you must eq, you must! Try these tips to maximize your eq chops:

Use Subtractive EQ

This is a big one: Use the eq to remove frequencies you don't want rather than accenting those you like. The most common usage of this trick is to remove the fundamental—the lowest portion—of the sound you're working on. This technique will emphasize the harmonics. For best results, you'll need at least a quasi-parametric (or a 10-band graphic). Start by boosting the eq at about 100 Hz, and sweep the frequency select control upwards. When you hit the fundamental, the sound should get markedly louder. Once you find it, try cutting a few dB.

Look for the Ugly Sounds

In the same way that you look for the fundamental by boosting an eq and then sweeping frequency, try doing what I call "looking for the ugly sounds." Each of us has our own sonic preferences. For me, the range around 1 kHz to 3 kHz is quite offensive, especially on guitars. For you, the ugly sounds may dwell elsewhere. In any case, look for them by boosting the eq and sweeping the frequency or by trying various faders on a graphic; once you find the offending frequency range, you can reduce or even remove it.

Use EQ to Minimize Noise

In the U.S., line current is 120 volts and 60 Hz. Take a wild guess what the frequency of ground loop hum is. That's right, 60 Hz. If you have a hum problem you can't kill any other way, you might try cutting a bit at 60 Hz. You'll get best results with a full parametric eq, set for minimum band width—you want to remove the hum only.

Attack the Mud

There is sonic mud around 400 Hz, so that's the first place I begin cutting if my mix is a bit murky. Try this on keyboard pads, guitars, voices—you name it. Long, sustained sounds often need the most help; short, percussive sounds can survive some mud.

Compensate for Your Recorder

A great use of eq is to compensate for changes in sound that normally occur during the recording process. On analog tape machines, even very expensive ones, there is usually a slight loss of extreme high end, say about 15 kHz. With experimentation, you can find an eq setting that will let you print just a bit hot at the frequencies you know you're going to lose. Since all machines sound different (not to mention all mixers), you'll really have to experiment to find an appropriate compensating eq.

Similarly, digital recorders may sound different to you, especially after years of recording analog. (Really, the digital recorder is probably more accurate in terms of frequency response—what goes in is what comes out.) You may find that warming up the low end, particularly of drums and bass, will help you achieve familiar results. In this case, notice that you'll be compensating in order to recreate sonic shortcomings that sound good to you.

EQ in Context

A very common eq mistake is to eq each sound in isolation: You solo the kick drum and eq it, then you solo the snare and eq it, then you solo the bass and eq it, etc. By the time you get around to listening to your whole mix, you've really made a mess. Just because a sound is great when soloed doesn't mean it will sound good in the track. The better way to deal with eq is to solo the sound and eq it, and then to check the sound in context—surrounded by the rest of the track.

Very often, a sound that is really ugly on its own is perfect in the track. A great example of this is the electric 12-string guitar. One of my favorite 12-string electrics sounds terrible on its own, but in a track it provides just the lift I want.

Boost Signal, Not Noise

Another common mistake is to try to boost a sound in a frequency that isn't there. Bass guitars don't have much above 5 kHz, so cranking the eq at 10 kHz only boosts noise. If exteme eq settings don't seem to do much, you've probably found an "empty" frequency band—the sound you're trying to eq doesn't have much energy at this frequency. In a case like this, you can try cutting other frequencies, or re-recording the part with a better sound to begin with.

Enhancer Tricks

Trick Number One

I use an enhancer (mine is a BBE) for several jobs in my studio. The first use is when tracking vocals or acoustic guitars. I route the signal through the enhancer, which is set to minimum effect — "lo" contour at 12 o'clock and "definition" set to 0 in "auto" mode — and listen. By switching the enhancer in and out, I can tell whether or not it's going to help. Very often, the enhancer doesn't do much, so I don't use it. Just as often, it makes whatever I'm recording sound better. If this is the case, I adjust the amount of enhancement to taste and record away.

Some studio rats I know use the enhancer on just about everything they record — anything that goes to tape goes through the enhancer. If you're the type that does this kind of thing, be careful! Using the same enhancer on every sound can lead to a sameness in the track that will be difficult to overcome later. This is why I use the enhancer only on instruments and voices that I want to stand out. If I use the enhancer for the lead vocal, I usually don't use it for the backups. If I use it for the electric guitars, I won't use it for the keyboards.

Trick Number Two
Use the enhancer subtly, because there is no way to undo the enhancer's effects. If you record the enhancer too hot, you'll have trouble at mix time. When in doubt, use less than you think you need; after all, you can always add more at mix time.

Trick Number Three
I almost always use the enhancer on the lead vocal at mix time. It seems to help the intelligibility of the vocal, which means the vocal can be turned down a bit in the mix. Since I usually record the lead vocal with a little enhancer, I only need to add a little bit now.

Trick Number Four
The final use I have for the enhancer is in making cassettes. I occasionally run my DAT outputs through the enhancer in order to brighten up a dull mix. I have found that the enhancer doesn't help much on good mixes; they already sound good! For my older mixes, the enhancer can often do the trick.

REVERBERATION
Maybe you have seen pictures of an anechoic chamber. The walls, floors and ceiling are deadened with specially shaped foam to kill off any reflections of sounds made within the chamber. As you might

guess, sounds made within such a chamber are dead—even very familiar sounds, such as your voice, will sound quite unusual. Move those same sounds to any other space, and they will change in character, depending on whether you are in a concert hall, a bathroom, at the beach or in a long corridor. The sounds reflected back by a particular environment are called *reverberation*.

In the studio, we use a reverb to simulate various sonic spaces, since having a concert hall at our disposal is unlikely. Even if we did have a concert hall ready and waiting for us to use, we would find very quickly that what works for a barbershop quartet won't work so well for a grunge-rock band. With a good digital reverb, we can have a large variety of sonic spaces to choose from in a very small unit.

Ideally, you should have at least two separate reverbs; one main reverb for vocals and overall ambience, and another unit just for the drums. (Most often, I end up dedicating the second reverb just to the snare drum). Now that reverb has become so inexpensive, it's very reasonable to have four, five or more reverbs. Right now, I have five reverbs, and I'm contemplating buying another. You may also have keyboards and drum machines with built-in reverbs, so it's a good idea to know how to manipulate them.

Reverb Types

The main types of reverb are room and plate. A *room* reverb is designed to simulate a room, and a *plate* reverb is designed to simulate a plate reverb. What's a plate reverb? Plate reverbs were an attempt to simulate natural reverberation with a mechanical device—a thin plate of metal about $3' \times 4'$, with a transducer (a type of speaker) and a pickup. Sound was sent into the plate by the transducer, and then returned by the pickup to the mixing console. The resulting sound wasn't exactly natural sounding; it had a pronounced high-frequency "sizzle," but the plate reverb sound became very popular for vocals.

The next most common reverb types are the gated reverb and the early reflection. *Gated* reverbs are most often used on drums, and they became hugely popular in the 1980s. I say hugely popular not only because everyone seemed to be using them, but also because of the huge sounds they created. Here's how they work: Let's say we're using a large room, long decay reverb on a snare drum. It sounds great as long as you only hear the snare—but add in the other instruments and the snare reverb mushes everything up. One solution might be to shorten the decay time or reduce the room size of the reverb. This will take care of the mush, but the sound just isn't the same. Here's where the gate comes in. Using the original too-big, too-long reverb, we insert a noise gate at the reverb's output. (A noise gate is like an auto on/off switch. Any sound below a certain amplitude threshold is turned off; cross the threshold, and the gate opens and lets the sound through. Gates will let you set how long the gate stays open, and how quickly it closes.) By setting the gate properly, we can make that huge reverb "stop" shortly after the initial snare hit, before the reverb gets a chance to mush up the other instruments. When the next snare hit arrives, some of the previous snare hit's reverb will be let in with the new, but the new ambience should mask the old.

Early reflection reverb is designed to simulate the first initial slap of reflected sound in a sonic space (plate, room, hall, etc.). This quick slap is heard very quickly after the initial sound, and the result is like being in a room with hard, reflective surfaces, such as glass or plaster. When you add this ambience to a sound, notice how the sound comes to life, especially when the early reflection is in stereo. Used subtly, early reflection adds depth to support instruments; in heavier doses, the early reflection sound can make lead instruments or vocals seem to jump out of the mix.

There are yet other variations of reverb, such as reverse room and plate, inverse room, etc. These reverb types are artificial creations—no natural rooms are able to cause a reverse reverb—but they are definitely worth exploring. Most of the parameters you will find in these reverb types will be familiar to you, once you understand how to adjust the main types of reverbs.

Using Predelay

On almost any reverb, there is a delay between the initial sound waiting to be effected and the input of the reverb. In other words, the snare hits, and the predelay makes the sound wait before it is sent to the reverb. (Notice that the predelay does not affect the dry, uneffected snare hit.) At first, predelay may seem like an unimportant parameter of a reverb, but with experimentation, you can discover how useful it is. Try this: Add a fairly heavy amount of medium size and time reverb (with a predelay time of zero) to a vocal, listening to just the voice and the reverb. Mix in the reverb heavy enough so that the reverb starts to cloud the intelligibility of the vocal. Next, add in the other instruments (drums, bass, etc.) from the track and notice just how hard it is to understand the singer without blasting the vocal in the mix. Now, try increasing the predelay time. What you should hear is an increase in the vocal's intelligiblity. Fine-tune this setting to suit the tempo of the song (consult the delay time/song temp chart in the section "Delay") and your ears. You may have to shorten the reverb's decay time to compensate for an extreme predelay setting, say 300 milliseconds or more.

Here's a neat trick for using predelay on synthesized strings. It works best on legato, single-note lines, say whole notes in ballad tempos. Use a predelay time that corresponds to a quarter or half note. If your reverb won't allow such a long predelay time, just hook up a delay before the reverb, set it to the time you want, and run the delayed signal (100 percent wet) to the reverb. Play the string part through the reverb, listening only to the reverb, then gradually add just a slight amount of the dry, unaffected string sound. By relying mostly on the reverb, you should get a very dreamy-feeling string sound.

Setting the Reverb Size

How big a room do you want your sound to be in? Do you want the men's room at the New York Hilton or the Taj Mahal? Your answer will tell you how to begin setting the reverb size.

Since the reverb is only simulating the differences in size, and since these simulations were arrived at by varying methods by different manufacturers, you'll need to spend some time listening to how your particular reverb changes as you adjust the size parameter. Here are some things to listen for: changes in decay time, tonal balance, front-to-back depth, and left-to-right width. Also notice how the "feel" of the room changes with size adjustments.

Reverb Technique

New Reverb Syndrome

Reverb neophytes always make the same mistake; they use way too much reverb on their mixes. I should know—the first tapes I played for people after I'd gotten my first good reverb elicited the following comment: "New reverb, huh?" Imagine my chagrin. As good as that new reverb sounded, my mixes had no punch; they were the sonic equivalent of buttermilk. The situation could have been worse: what if I'd had *two* new reverbs? Here's how to avoid getting caught too long in new reverb syndrome (NRS):

1. Not everything needs reverb. You may be surprised at how much clarity you gain by simply removing the reverb from supporting instruments.

2. Listen to recordings to hear how much reverb the pros use. Bear in mind that it's best to compare a song or track that is similar to the one you are working on.

3. Spend the most amount of reverb effort on the vocals. Once you have the vocal reverb set the way you like it, try turning the reverb output all the way down, then gradually reinsert reverb as you listen to the track.

4. Experiment. Try various reverb amounts, room sizes, reverb eq's, etc. If you make rough mixes, you can listen at a later time and decide which approach works best for you.

Mono Reverb

Now that stereo reverb is so common, we all tend to use it all the time. Every once in awhile, this leads to inappropriate sonic "slickness." If your aggressive alternative country rap track still sounds a bit too tame, try setting the vocal reverb returns to the center pan position, as opposed to left and right. This also works well for those old fifties and sixties rock, country and soul sounds.

Reverb EQ

Many reverbs have built-in equalization, which can be used to creatively shape the sound of the 'verb. (If your reverb doesn't have any eq, you can always plug the reverb's outputs into an external graphic equalizer or even into a spare pair of channels on your console.) Here's one possible trick: Use a separate reverb for the snare. Start with a really fat snare sound, with lots of meat in the low end. Now, add a long reverb. Notice how mushy the reverb sounds? Take out the mush by using a high-pass filter or simply turning the low eq down. With a little tweaking, you should be able to get the initial fat sound of the snare with a nice, long, sizzling tail. Don't forget to play with the predelay setting.

Preverb

This trick takes a little bit of work with your analog multitrack tape machine. The idea is to hear the reverb sound *before* the dry sound. First, record (on tape) the sound to be "preverbed." Next, flip the reel of tape over, so that the left reel is now on the right side, and vice versa. Once the tape is flipped, you'll have to reset any locate points, since the beginning of the song is now at the end of the tape, and the end is at the beginning. You will also find that the tape tracks have reversed — on an 8-track machine, track 1 is now track 8, track 2 is now track 7 and so on. For this reason, you'll have to be very careful not to accidentally erase any tracks you meant to keep. The next step is to run the backwards track into the reverb, and record just the reverb on an empty track (or tracks, for stereo). Finally, flip the reels back into their normal orientation, reset your locate points and play back. Sounds pretty cool, huh? You will, of course, need to experiment in order to get the effect you want.

Reverb Only

A neat effect, particularly for slower tempos, is to have an instrument that is 100 percent reverb — no dry sound whatsoever. This can make guitars sound lonelier and vocals ghostlier. Try some reverb eq to complete the picture.

Dry Only

The opposite of the above effect is no reverb — dry signal only. When I use this effect, it's usually a contrast to other elements or sections in the track. For example, a very dreamy sax sound with lots of reverb and delay contrasted with a totally dry lead vocal, or reverb on the verse vocal and the chorus vocal, but no reverb on the bridge vocal.

Riding the 'Verb

Let's say the vocal you're working with has a long, sustained note at the end of a chorus. Try gradually increasing the reverb send as the note sustains, so that by the end of the note, all you hear is reverb. If you "milk" the reverb this way, you can intensify the effect of the sustained note. This trick also works well with instruments, such as guitars and brass. You can also turn the reverb send down for verses, up a little bit for the prechoruses, and up some more for choruses. If you want to get really slick, you can automate these moves through MIDI, leaving your hands and mind free for other chores.

Changing the Reverb

This is similar to the trick I outlined above. Use a small room for the verses and a long one for the chorus. Once again, you can have MIDI handle the actual work.

DELAY

Delay is the most basic of electronic effects. In concept, it's simple: The dry sound is played, and sometime later, the same sound is heard again. The first way this was accomplished in the studios of the 1950s was by using an extra three-head (erase, record, play) tape machine. The dry signal was fed into the machine, recorded by the record head, and played back by the playback head. Since there is a physical distance between the record and playback heads, the playback signal is delayed. During a mix, the delay tape machine was loaded with a full reel of tape, and set into record — when it ran out of tape, the reel was rewound and started again. Hopefully, you didn't run out of tape in the middle of a perfect mix! Controlling the time of the delay created was iffy — if the machine had two speeds, say 7.5 and 15 ips, you could have two delay times. This setup allowed for only one repeat of the dry sound. Someone figured out that taking the delayed signal and feeding it back into the delay tape machine gave more than one repeat — in fact, there would be infinite repeats if the fed back level was set too high. An interesting byproduct of this feedback loop was that tape hiss was fed back into the machine along with the delayed signal, creating a weird, spacey sound. You've heard this sound on any number of fifties and sixties sci-fi movies and TV shows, from *Cat Women of the Moon* and *It Came From Outer Space* to *The Outer Limits* and even *Dr. Who*.

Soon, there were specialized tape-delay machines, like the Echoplex, which were designed to be delay machines only. The Echoplex used a tape loop rather than reels, and delay time was controlled by allowing the user to slide the playback head back and forth — closer to the record head for short delays, and farther away for very long delays (more than a second). A knob labeled *repeat* controlled the feedback amount, and an additional feature allowed the erase head to be defeated. Once the tape loop came back to the starting point (a minute or so later), sounds that were a minute or so old started appearing along with what was being currently delayed. Very psychedelic, and just in time for the sixties.

These tape delays had problems. Since they used tape, they were noisy, and each repeated delay added more and more noise. The tapes needed to be replaced from time to time, and since these were mechanical devices, repairs were inevitable.

Nowadays, the tape delay has been replaced by the digital delay. Early digital delays were very limited and expensive, but now, even a cheap delay outperforms those first pieces. (There have also been analog delays, but they can be considered to be functionally the same as digital delays.) Here are the basic parameters of a digital delay:

1. Delay time. Most delays express delay time in milliseconds — 1,000 milliseconds equals one second. The longer the delay available, the better.

2. Feedback (or *repeat*, or *regeneration*). As mentioned above, feedback sends a portion of the delayed signal back into the delay input. Set this level high enough and the delay will repeat infinitely.

3. Depth and Speed. These are low-frequency oscillator (LFO) settings. The output of the LFO is used to change the delay setting; depth sets how much the LFO changes the delay, and speed sets how often the LFO sweeps. The LFO is continuously shifting, and this causes the delay to shorten and lengthen, creating pitch changes in the delayed signal.

That's it. You may find other parameters to adjust on the fancier delays, such as phase inversion (try it and listen), but that's all there is to using a delay. Here are some tricks to try.

Flanging, Chorusing and Doubling

By using the LFO to vary the delay time, you can create your own flanging, chorusing and doubling effects. The main difference between these three is the basic delay setting. Use around 10 ms for flanging, around 25 ms for chorusing, and around 45 ms for doubling. I say *around* because you'll need to fine-tune this setting to your choice. The LFO depth will need to be set differently, too; a depth setting of 100 percent LFO may be appropriate for flanging, but at higher delay settings, the pitch change caused by the LFO will be too extreme. Feedback should be set very low or off for chorusing and doubling but as high as possible for flanging. The balance between the effect and un-effected sound (dry) should be set from 30 to 50 percent for chorusing and doubling, but for flanging, you might want to try as much as 100 percent effect. If your delay has a phase reversal switch, you may want to try it to see how it sounds.

Rhythmic Delay

Try setting the delay so that it occurs in the tempo of the song you're working on. If you've got several delays, set one up to repeat on quarter notes, one on eighths and one on sixteenths. With a little experimentation, you'll be able to find a combination that works for you. Once you've gotten used to quarter notes (and eighths and sixteenths), try using triplets. (I like quarter-note triplets for solo instruments.) Setting the appropriate delay times for various tempos is not too difficult; in fact, some delays allow you to tap on a pedal to set the delay time. Others can set their own delay time if they are receiving midi tempo from a sequencer or drum machine. For delays that need to be set the old-fashioned way, you can use your ears—just turn up the feedback so that the delay repeats many times. This way, you'll be able to hear if the repeats get ahead of the beat (increase delay time) or go behind (decrease delay time). If you have a calculator handy, you can use this formula to figure the exact delay time:

> *60,000 milliseconds (one minute) divided by tempo (beats per minute) equals quarter-note delay time (in any time signature where a quarter note gets one beat; for example, 4/4, 3/4, 5/4, 7/4).*

Divide the quarter-note delay time by two to get the eighth-note delay time and by four to get the sixteenth-note delay time. To get triplets, multiply the quarter-note delay time by two, giving you the half-note delay time. Divide this number by three for quarter-note triplets, by six for eighth-note triplets, and by twelve for sixteenth-note triplets. For example, at a tempo of 100 beats per minute, you'd divide 60,000 by 100, giving a quarter-note delay setting of 600 milliseconds. Divide this by two, and we get an eighth-note delay time of 300 milliseconds; by four and we have the sixteenth-note delay time of 150 milliseconds.

For triplets, double the quarter-note delay time to get 1,200 milliseconds. Divide by three to get 400 milliseconds, the quarter-note triplet delay time; by six to get 200 milliseconds, the eighth-note triplet delay time; by twelve to get 100 milliseconds, the sixteenth-note triplet delay time.

(By the way, I have often used quarter-note triplet delay times, seldom used eighth-note delay times, and never intentionally used a sixteenth-note triplet delay time. The reason for this is that I usually set shorter delay times by ear, listening to how a particular setting feels.)

Here's a trick for making a simple guitar (or keyboards, or . . .) lines interesting. Set your delay so that it repeats two and a half beats after you play a note. If you play on beat one, it should sound like this: *ONE* and two *AND* three and four and. Be sure that you have set the feedback "off," so that the delay plays only one repeat. Turn the volume of the delay up as loud as the instrument you are playing. Next, start playing any quarter-note line. Surprise! At higher tempos, this trick can make you sound like Albert Lee; at slower tempos, you can get more of the Edge vibe happening.

Using Multiple Delays

Some delay units have more than one delay line. By sending in a signal, you get two separate delay times back. Usually these two delays will appear split, one on the left, and one on the right. Sometimes, there are several delay lines (usually called *multi-tap* delays) that appear in a stereo spread. You can treat these multi delays as if they were several separate delays, with a few important differences. First, since there is usually only one input, you will obviously be able to use the delays only as a group: You can't send guitar to one delay and keyboard to the other. (This will also be true for delays that appear to have a stereo input. The stereo input is there for convenience only—stereo input is summed internally and fed into the delay lines. This also applies to most reverbs with stereo inputs. Read your manual carefully.) Second, some parameters will affect both delays. Most common is the feedback control. The drawback here is that you can't make one delay repeat forever and one repeat only once; for that trick, you'll need two separate delays. Third, multiple delay lines may have some special tricks unique to the unit you are using. This is an advantage, so be sure to make yourself familiar with whatever special games your delay can play.

PITCH TRANSPOSERS

This effect can take a sound and change its pitch, up or down, usually by as much as an octave—instant harmonies can be created, as well as more subtle effects like chorusing that doesn't "move." The main controls on a pitch transposer are tune, fine-tune, delay and regeneration. The tune parameter is usually expressed in semitones or musical intervals, such as seven semitones/perfect fifth. Fine-tune gives smaller adjustments, usually in *cents*—there are 100 cents to a semitone. The delay parameter is the same as predelay; it lets you delay the signal a bit before you effect it. Notice that there will always be some predelay when using a pitch transposer, since a good bit of time is needed to process a signal to a different pitch. Regeneration works the same in a pitch transposer as in a delay: Effected signal is routed back to the input of the effect. On a pitch transposer, this causes some interesting effects. Sounds that are being transposed slightly flat will repeat with regeneration (the delay setting determines how fast the repeats occur), and each repeat will be lower in pitch. Transpose slightly sharp, and the repeats will cascade up in pitch.

Nonmoving Chorus

The most common use for a pitch transposer is as a nonmoving chorus. It works great on vocals and instruments, by slightly detuning the sound you're working on. Set the tune parameter to unison or *0*, the fine-tune to ±1, the delay to minimum and the regeneration off. Mix in the effect with the original sound, and adjust levels to taste. If your pitch transposer allows you to set two different intervals, you can set one sharp by one cent and the other flat by one cent; pan the two left and right, and you've got stereo chorus.

Parallel Harmony

Pitch transposers can also be used to provide parallel harmonies, such as a fifth, to a sound. If your pitch transposer allows more than one interval, you can even construct a parallel chord by setting one interval to a third above and another to a fifth above or a fourth below. You'll need to be aware of a few things. The farther away from unison, the worse the pitch transposer will sound. Also, single notes will work better than chords in most instances, so you'll probably end up using this effect most for solo instruments. I have used this effect on vocals, but in a not-too-obvious way: I needed to make some background shouts sound thicker, so I added some lower intervals to the existing shouts. The crowd seemed to double in size and complexity.

Here's a chart showing the relationship between semitones and musical intervals:

Semitones	Interval
1	(half step)
2	second
3	minor third
4	major third
5	perfect fourth
6	augmented fourth, flatted fifth, or tri-tone
7	perfect fifth
8	augmented fifth
9	sixth
10	dominant seventh
11	major seventh
12	octave

Moving Pitch Transposing

As I mentioned before, you can cause the sound being sent through a pitch transposer to cascade up or down by using the regeneration control. This works very well on percussion sounds, such as snares and toms. If you set the transposer's interval slightly flat with some regeneration added, you'll hear the snare drum's pitch drop after the initial hit. You'll need to fine-tune the interval, regeneration and delay settings to your taste. More extreme effects work great on dance material.

"Intelligent" Harmony

Some pitch shifters can create harmonies that will stay within the scale tones of the key you are playing in. You have to set a key and select a scale, then the device will automatically choose the "correct" intervals; so you'll hear your original note, and two other notes selected by the device. Intelligent shifters work as they are supposed to as long as you give them only one note to harmonize — any polyphonic playing will mess them up, and the resulting sounds will be anything but harmonic! As always, if you like this kind of thing, feel free to use it.

STUDIO MONITORS

Ask ten engineers or producers their opinions on studio monitors, and you'll hear several different opinions—one set of ears loves the same speakers that another can't stand. Interestingly enough, everyone finds something wrong with even their favorite monitors. Here are some tips to help you choose some decent monitors and better utilize the ones you have.

Use Good Monitors

First, you need to understand that using good monitors is very important, since you'll be making sonic decisions at every turn based on what you hear. If your monitors have a flaw, your recordings will suffer. The bad news is that all monitors have flaws; the good news is that you can compensate once you get used to your particular speakers. There's only one way to get used to a particular pair of monitors, and that's to use them. It's also helpful to listen to recordings you are very familiar with on your speakers: You'll then have some idea of how they behave.

Choose the Correct Size Monitors

If your studio is small, you don't need big monitors. Even if your studio is big, you'll need at least one pair of *near-field* monitors. Near-field monitors are small to medium-sized; usually the low-frequency driver is 8″ or less. Most often, monitors of this sort are two-way.

Place Your Speakers Properly

Where you place your speakers has a huge effect on how they sound. Most home-studio monitoring is done with the listener's head fairly close to the speakers—within two or three feet—and at ear level. This is called *near-field* monitoring, for obvious reasons. It also helps to have the speakers closer to the listener's ears than to any walls; this helps minimize the effects of the room. Try this experiment: Listen to a bass-heavy track through your monitors and move your speakers to different locations, starting with a location as far away from the walls (or floor or ceiling) as possible. Next, move the speaker to the floor, then on the floor next to a wall, and finally on the floor in a corner. You should be amazed at the differences. If not, you are a tin-eared goober and you should go back to reading *Guns & Ammo*. You'll also want to try different ways of setting up your speakers: standing up or lying down. If you end up putting your spakers on their side, try positioning the tweeters (high-frequency drivers) toward the outside.

So . . . you have the speakers at ear level, and two or three feet away from your head, but your room is so small that the speakers are still pretty close to the wall. Try, try, try to get them as far away from the wall as you can. Try another experiment. You'll need an assistant. Start by listening to the best-recorded CD you own—the one you would take to listen to on a deserted island. As you listen, have your assistant move the speakers very close to the wall, and then move them farther and farther away. The differences will be small, but you'll hear them. You may also find a position when the sound seems to "lock"; if so, you've just found a great place to keep your monitors.

By now, reality has set in. The perfect place for your monitors is so far into the room that you have no room to work. Sigh. Put them back toward the wall, but only as much as you really need; every inch helps.

Next, look at what your speakers are sitting on. If you're like me, you've erected some sort of shelf over your console. Great. There's only one problem: The shelf itself (nice inner rhyme, eh?) resonates, adding a subtle smearing to the sound of your speakers. The cheap way out (always my first choice) is to acoustically isolate the speakers from the shelf with some nonresonant material. Foam rubber works great. I've even used magazines and folded towels. Once again, experiment.

The wall behind the speakers will affect the sounds you hear, since reflections will be created by such a large, flat, hard surface. You can deaden the wall with an old blanket or quilt. Better yet, spend about twenty dollars for a piece of sculpted foam rubber.

Use a Good Power Amp

How you power the speakers is important, too. Use the cleanest, most powerful amp you can afford. In home studios, you can get by with as little as 20 watts per channel, but you'll notice the difference when you switch to a more powerful amp. You'll also find that your tweeters will be more likely to blow up from being underpowered than overpowered. The reason is that as a low-powered amp reaches the limit of its capabilities, it distorts, turning the signal into a square wave. Tweeters hate square waves (the title of my new screenplay). A big amp won't distort when you turn it up.

That brings up another point: Watch your volume. Speakers that are accurate at one level are less accurate when they are turned up too loud, and you'd be shocked at how little volume it takes to change the sound of a speaker. There are exceptions, however. When you are tracking an instrument, you may need a higher level to get the performer excited. In that case, go to it, but be careful not to blow up your speakers.

Use More Than One Pair of Monitors

I like to have a few monitors to choose from when I'm working. When I'm tracking, I want a monitor that I can listen to for a long period of time without going deaf. When I'm mixing, I check my work on these same monitors by comparing to another pair or two. Each of the three pairs is different—one set is critical in the midrange, but nonexistent in the bass. The next set has a much better extended high and low end than the first pair, but is tricky in the middle. The final pair is set designed to act like car stereo speakers. They sound really awful, but there have been circumstances that listening to them saved a mix.

How to Audition Speakers in a Store

When you go out to buy monitors, try listening to your desert island disk, and be sure to listen to all of the speakers at the same volume level—if one set is louder than the others, it will almost always "sound" better. I also find that it helps to compare only two speakers at once. Once I know that I prefer one over the other, I then compare my current preference to a new pair. If you can, try to get the store to allow you to return the speakers if you don't like them once you get them home, or perhaps to let you try out a demo pair at home. Even so, don't be surprised if the speakers you loved when you bought them sound less than perfect six months later. That six months educated your ears—now you may have to go out and get more monitors!

THE WELL-TEMPERED DAT MACHINE

The Advantages of DAT

You've got a DAT (digital audio tape) machine, don't you? If you don't, you probably should—it's an extremely convenient, high-performance medium for mixing. Even though I have both a DAT recorder and an analog two-track, I use the DAT for nearly every mix I do. Here are the main advantages as far as I see them:

1. Tape costs. A two-hour DAT tape costs a little more than ten dollars. The same amount of time in ¼" tape is closer to sixty dollars. With tape costs so low, I can make lots of mixes of the same track.

2. Storage space. The two-hour DAT takes up less space than a normal analog cassette tape. The four 10½" reels of ¼" tape take up much more room.

3. Convenience of operation. Just pop in a DAT and you're ready to go. With a reel-to-reel two-track, you've got to thread the machine. It's not too tough, but the DAT is clearly easier to use.

4. No tape noise. No way around it, analog tape makes noise. Noise reduction can essentially eliminate analog tape hiss, but it's not in common use on two-track machines.

5. Endless copies. When you make a dub of an analog master, you increase the noise level. (The noise already on the master gets recorded onto the dub, which adds its own noise. With each new generation, from master to dub to dub of a dub, the noise gets worse.) With DAT, you can *theoretically* make endless copies of copies, all of which will be indistinguishable from each other. More on the theoretical part later.

6. Dynamic range and freqency response. With analog tape, the dynamic range of material being recorded is reduced—compressed. (This is not always a bad thing.) DAT maintains the dynamic range of what you're recording, so much so that you may not be able to tell the mix from the multitrack playback. The same sort of thing applies to the frequency response of analog tape vs. DAT. Analog tape does change the sound (again, this may not be a bad thing), and DAT by its nature gives back what goes in.

7. Expense. In addition to tape costs, the actual cost of a good DAT machine is less than that of a competitive analog two-track. By *competitive*, I mean a machine that sounds so good that you'd consider using it instead of the DAT machine. To my ears, the only two tracks that compete with DAT machines (and may be superior in many cases) are pro level ½", 30 ips machines, which are quite expensive to purchase, operate and maintain, as well as taking up a lot of floor space in a studio.

Working With DAT

So, you need to have a DAT machine, even if your multitrack machine is a four-track cassette job. Nowadays, you can buy a fine DAT recorder for well under a thousand dollars, which should last you for years with a little care. Once you've made your purchase, you'll find that dealing with a DAT machine is quite a bit different from handling any other type of tape recorder, audio or video. Video? Well, a DAT machine is more like a video recorder than you might know—both types of machine use a rotating head that "scans" the tape at an angle. Instead of a contiguous tape track (made by a stationary head, like on your analog multitrack), which looks like this: --------------, the rotating head creates a track with each rotation of the head, resulting in a pattern like this: //////////////. The advantage to this arrangement is that more data can be put onto less tape. (Analog tape needs wider tracks than digital. Since digital is recording only 0s and 1s, there is no need for fidelity on the tape. The tape tracks on an analog two-track are about 3/32″ wide for each channel, left and right. On a DAT machine, the track width is closer to that of a human hair. Additionally, a single DAT track carries both the left and right signals.) This similarity to video causes some interesting problems, for example, recording on an analog machine is nearly instantaneous—just punch in. For a DAT machine, you need to start recording a few seconds early, like a video recorder. Also, just as it can be a pain to find a specific recording on a video tape, locating specific recordings on a DAT can be quite annoying. To solve this and other problems, DAT manufacturers created "id's" to mark sections of the tape.

There are three types of DAT id. First, and most important is the "start" id. This id is usually written at the very beginning of a recording, although it can be written anywhere you like on the tape. For example, if you have twenty-two songs on a two-hour DAT, you can have a start id for the beginning of each song. You might also have a start id in the middle of song number twelve, say at the second verse. The total number of start id's on your tape would then be twenty-three. When you record one selection after another, the DAT machine can be set to automatically number the start id's in sequence: 1, 2, 3 and so on. Start id's can also be written or erased without affecting any music recorded on the tape, although the *write protect* tab on the DAT cassette itself will have to be set properly. (When the tab covers the small hole on the back edge of the

DAT cassette, recording is possible. When the hole is uncovered, recording is not possible.)

Depending on your machine, there will be occasions when start id's get out of sequence or the start id is written without a number — perhaps you've erased a start id, or perhaps you've added one in between two others. In either case, you can use a feature called "renumber" to put all of the numbers in sequence. Once you press the appropriate button, the machine will rewind to the top of the tape and begin "looking" at the start id's. As long as they are numbered in sequence, the machine will wind on to the next start id. Once an out-of-sequence or numberless id is found, the machine will rewrite the id and give it the proper number. This process continues until the end of the tape or until an "end" id is reached.

The "end" id is the second type of id used on a DAT machine. The idea of the end id is to let you easily find the last recorded bit on your tape without a lot of searching. Usually, the procedure is to write an end id after you've finished recording; once it's there, the machine will not play or fast forward past that point on that tape — it will simply stop. If you enter *record* at this point, the end id will be erased. *Use caution!* Writing an end id will *erase* any audio that was previously recorded at that location on the tape. Also, I have had occasions where my machine allowed me to only partially erase an end id. (I must have "found" the id from fast forward; even though the machine stopped the tape, it must have stopped it past the beginning of the end id.) When I tried to play the tape back, there was enough of an end id to stop the machine dead in its tracks, even though the mix I wanted to hear was past the partially erased end id. The solution? I had to go into *record* long enough to erase the remaining bit of end id and stop in time to avoid erasing the first bit of my mix. Now I'm very careful to erase the entire end id.

The last type of id is the "skip" id, and I've only used it a few times. The purpose of the skip id is to tell the machine, "When you see me, go into fast forward until you find the next start id, then start playing again." It's useful as a kind of edit, to cut out material you don't want to hear. Most machines can be set to ignore skip id's.

DAT machines do have some compatibility problems. Some of these problems are simply annoyances; few early machines wrote "absolute" time on the tape, but most newer machines do. Absolute time is a great feature to have — it's like a tape counter that doesn't drift. However, in order for absolute time to be written on a tape, you must always record on a machine that has this feature. Once you use a nonabsolute time machine to record, the tape will revert to a normal tape-counter-type display at the point you began recording. Some early machines write start and other id's that new machines don't fully recognize, and vice versa. In cases like this, you can usually do a renumber and straighten things out, or simply erase the old id's and "manually" write new ones.

A very serious incompatibility problem can occur between DAT machines, and the worst part is that it's very unpredictable. If you have a VCR, you've probably noticed a "tracking" control. This control is an adjustment to match the tracking of the VCR head to the tape. In most cases, you can play a tape made on another VCR without any adjustments, but occasionally, you will need to turn the tracking knob to compensate for a tape that plays a bit fuzzily. I have had similar misalignments occur with a DAT tape recorded on one machine and played back on another. The big problem was that the machine's misalignment kept changing, getting a little bit worse from month to month. I finally had to get rid of the machine, but what about my tapes? The only cure was for me to find a machine that could play the "bad" tapes, and make a digital copy with my new machine. If you have a problem like this, try playing the problem tapes on a number of machines until you find one that can handle the misalignment. If necessary, go to the store you bought the machine from and try as many DAT machines as you can. Whatever you do, don't erase your bad tapes until you've made a satisfactory copy: even if you can't find a machine that will play them today, perhaps you will tomorrow.

The standard enemies of tape machines apply to DAT machines, perhaps even more so. Try to avoid dusty environments, as well as high humidity and temperature extremes. If you have a portable DAT machine, be very careful about physical shocks. Even though the machine was built to travel, it is still quite delicate. DAT machine heads need to be cleaned occasionally, but there is a bit of disagreement over whether cleaning can damage the machine. It's best to get recommendations from the manufacturer of your machine.

Things to Remember

Here are some other important things to remember when using a DAT machine.

Record as Hot as You Can

If you're used to analog machines, you know that if you record a louder and louder level, eventually you will get distortion as the tape overloads. This overload occurs gradually. At first, the signal compresses just a bit — what you give the tape comes back slightly squished on the loudest portions. If the signal is increased, more of the signal will be compressed, the louder sections more so than the softer. Eventually, the tape saturates, and the result is distortion.

On digital machines, the onset of distortion is anything but gradual. Right up to the limit, there is no compression. Cross the limit of the digital medium, and you'll get an *overload* — a very harsh, unmusical sound. Under no circumstances do you want to have an overload on your tape. When DAT machines first appeared, everyone I know simply recorded at a level several dB below the point where an overload would occur. The problem with this scheme is that the DAT medium loses resolution (detail) as the level drops. (For you techno-nerds out there, a 16-bit signal loses one bit of resolution for each 6 dB drop in level.) For this reason, it's important to record just as hot as you can.

You'll find that the meters on most DAT machines are calibrated to show a signal hotter than it really is during *record*. Very often, I'll get an overload indication while I'm recording, but on playback, there are no overloads to be found. You'll need to experiment with your machine to find out if this situation applies. In any case, if there is an overload indication during playback, you've recorded too hot.

DAT Tape Care

DAT tapes appear to be less sensitive to magnetic fields than normal analog tape; all the same, avoid the usual problem areas such as unshielded speakers, telephones and TVs, as well as those pesky refrigerator magnets. Always keep DAT tapes in their protective case. *Do not* keep DAT tapes in your car — they will die very quickly from the sunlight and temperature extremes. Purses and pockets are also bad places to keep DATs. If you're going to be carrying DAT tapes around, there are storage cases that give additional protection from the elements. It's best to keep tapes rewound to the top.

Avoid Nonrecorded Blanks

A common mistake that beginning DAT users make is to leave non-recorded blank sections between recordings. The problem is that the machine will see these nonrecorded sections and think that it has found the end of the tape; some machines may even refuse to play past a nonrecorded blank that's a few seconds too long. The machine's behavior may make you believe you've found the end of your recordings, meaning you may start recording at a point before the end of your recordings. Guess what? You'll erase one of your masters.

What you do want is to have *recorded* blank sections after each song—three to five seconds is optimum. To do this, simply record a few seconds of silence after each mix. Most machines have a feature that does this automatically for you—*auto record mute*. Check your manual for details.

Making Copies

You must make copies of your masters. Just think: How much money do you have invested in your master mixes? How much money and time would it cost to redo all of your mixes if you lost your master DAT(s) or if it were destroyed in a fire (God forbid)? *Make copies of your masters and store them in a different location.*

When you make copies, make digital copies. The reason for this is that you will be bypassing the conversion processes (digital to analog, analog back to digital) which can cause deterioration of the signal. This loss is similar to, but not nearly as extreme as, the generation loss that occurs when analog copies are made. Digital copies are theoretically identical to the original, but the reality is that errors do occur each time a copy is made. These errors can come from dust on one of the tapes, or a cable that's iffy, or perhaps a power surge. (I've also experienced tapes that were bad right out of the box.) Usually, these errors are inaudible, and so they are little cause for concern. Still, it's a good idea to check your copies carefully.

Making digital copies is complicated by the "serial copy management system," which was implemented to prevent consumer machines from being able to make an unlimited number of perfect copies. If your machine has SCMS, you will be allowed to make only one digital copy of any of your tapes. The problem gets worse if you have a tape that was made on a consumer machine that was built before SCMS was implemented. Some of those machines put a "copy status uncertain" message on any tapes you make on them. When you try to make a copy with an SCMS machine, you get a "prohibited" message—no copies allowed.

There is a way around all this: buy or borrow a professional machine. You'll need a second DAT machine to make copies anyway, so find a friend to borrow a machine from in exchange for use of your machine. As long as one is a pro machine, you can make endless copies of your tapes. Just use the SCMS machine as the player and the pro machine as the recorder.

What is a pro machine? Pro machines offer multiple sampling rates for recording (see below) and usually have both standard digital interfaces: AES/EBU and the consumer S/P DIF. (You will probably use S/P DIF most often unless you are interfacing with other pro digital devices.) Pro machines are SCMS-free—you can make copy after copy without hassle. Some even allow you to make tapes that prohibit anyone else from making a copy. Finally, a pro machine usually has + 4 dB balanced inputs and outputs as well as the semi-pro -10 dB unbalanced connections.

Sample-Rate Hell

The standard sample rate for consumer DAT machines is 48 kHz. This means that the DAT machine makes 48,000 sonic "snapshots" every second for each of two stereo channels, resulting in a total of 96,000 snapshots per stereo second. (Whew!) When you play back these snapshots, it's something like flipping through a deck of cards, each card having a picture drawn on it that advances the action— you see a mini movie. Didn't you have one of these decks of cards when you were a kid? If not, stop reading and go directly to Toys 'R' Us. Anyway, flipping through the digital snapshots results in a signal that can be converted into sound. The sampling rate tells the machine how fast to flip the cards. You may have noticed that the sample rate for CDs is 44.1 kHz. Notice the incompatibility? This is a continuation of the effort to discourage the unlimited copying of commercial products; a consumer DAT machine operating at 48 kHz can't make a digital copy of a 44.1 kHz CD.

Consumer DAT machines will play back a 44.1 DAT; they just can't record at that sample rate. Pro machines, on the other hand, can record and play back at either frequency.

What does all of this mean to you? Simply that if you are recording home demos that will most likely not be used on a CD, you can record at 48 kHz. This means that you can operate with a less expensive consumer machine. If the work you do regularly goes to CD or if you need to digitally interface with other pro gear, you may need to have the 44.1 kHz recording capability. By the way, if you have a 48 kHz master that needs to get to CD, it's no big deal to convert it to 44.1 kHz. Just find someone with a digital hard-disk editor, such as Sound Tools on the Macintosh, and pay them to do the job.

Machine Eats Tapes?

There's nothing quite like the nausea you'll feel if your DAT machine eats a one-of-a-kind master. Let's see, there's the "Ohmygod, that mix was perfect. . . ." and the "How much will *this* cost to get repaired?" and then the "Now I won't have my DAT machine for the next *xxxx* weeks." Try to relax. Depending on the situation, you may get away with virtually no damage. I've found most tape eating to be the result of a faulty tape rather than a broken machine. I have also been able to rescue an eaten tape and have it live to play long enough to make a copy.

Before going any further, if you are not extremely handy and sensitive to machinery, or if your machine is under warranty, *stop*. Take your machine to a repair shop (hope it's a good one) and beg them to be ultracareful about removing the tape. If you're lucky, the tech will be able to rethread the cassette and get it to play long enough to make a copy. Once you get a copy, throw the bad DAT away.

If you are bold and willing to take the consequences of your own actions, you might decide to try to disengage the eaten tape yourself. *If you mess things up, it's your fault, not mine!* Get it? OK. The one time I had a tape get eaten, I had opened the tape door and pulled out the cassette. Unfortunately, the actual tape was steaming out of the DAT cassette and into the bowels of my DAT machine. I *gently* pulled on the tape, being careful not to touch it with my fingers (I used cotton swabs to touch the tape), until I felt resistance from whatever was catching the tape inside the machine. I then closed and reopened the tape door. This released the tape. All I had to do was to open the protective door on the DAT cassette (use your fingernails to release the catches) and carefully wind the tape back into the cassette, being sure not to crease the tape. When I played the tape again, it got eaten again — I freed the tape again and tried to play it one more time. It worked long enough for me to make a copy. Yea!

If you have a situation like this, and the tape is creased, you may be out of luck — the creased section may not ever play properly again. The only recourse you have is to make a copy of the selections that aren't creased and throw the damaged cassette away.

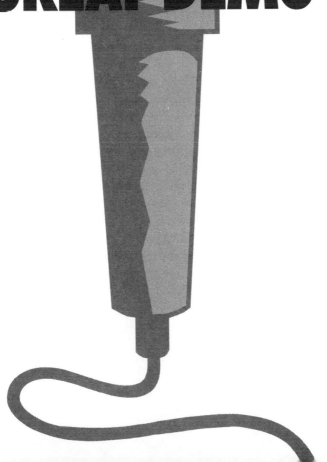

PART TWO

FOUR STEPS TO A GREAT DEMO

Step One

PREPARATION

ARRANGEMENT

There's lots of important work to do before you start recording. You need to decide on the tempo of the song, the key, the lengths of the various sections, and the style you want the demo to be. All of this together is called the *arrangement*. Skip this step at your peril! If you don't plan carefully, you'll probably end up doing the whole thing over again. This may not matter to you; if you're in a band, trial and error is one of the best ways to work out an arrangement. If this is the case, be sure to tape every rehearsal with a hand-held cassette machine or a blaster. You don't have to tape every moment (who has time to listen to every second of a rehearsal!), just record every musical variation you're considering. It also helps to announce a description of what you're about to do before you record each section, such as: "Here's another possible bridge idea; it's seven bars instead of eight," and so on. This type of arranging is really part of the songwriting process. You songwriters out there will also find the hand-held tape recorder invaluable if you don't already use it.

Making decisions regarding the arrangement is really important, since you'll be setting the course for the entire demo you're about to do. There are lots of factors to consider in each decision, but the common factor is to do what you feel. There's a trap here, especially if you're the type who loves all your own ideas simply because you came up with them, or if you're not in the habit of continually learning new things. If you always do what you feel, but you always feel the same old things, you'll quickly find yourself in a rut. The same sort of rut will occur if you're unable to accept ideas from others. So, beware. Do what you feel, but be open to new ideas, no matter where they come from.

Match the Demo to the Song

Usually, a song is best suited to one style of music. Occasionally, you'll write a song that could be rock or country, or a song that could be pop and almost anything else, but usually the song will suggest the style of the demo. Once again, if you are a band or an artist, you'll have a bit of leeway in this regard, but still, the fundamental idea applies. Songwriters who are writing with the idea of getting a cover should know that their songs will have a much better chance of being considered by an artist if the style of demo is appropriate. You'll have no luck presenting an r&b-style demo to a country artist. You'll also find that a melody or lyric that sounds great in a pop demo may need to be slightly modified to work in a country demo.

So, you must match the demo to the song by first choosing the proper genre, be it rock, r&b, rap, country, pop, new age, folk, alternative, polka or Balinese Gamelan music. Within each genre, you'll find that there are several styles, and that these styles are constantly shifting, depending on what's popular and what's not.

Choosing Musical Models

Unless you know precisely what style you want your demo to be, it's a good idea to find a recording (or two or three) to base your demo on. This doesn't mean you should copy everything about this recording and simply transfer your song into it—I just mean that you can get arrangement ideas that are appropriate to the genre by listening to recordings that have already been successful. From one recording, you might find a groove that would be appropriate for your song. This will give you a good starting point; just copy the basic idea of the groove and then modify it to suit your purposes. From another recording, you might hear some sounds you like, and from a third, you might hear a cool vocal arrangement. As long as you use these ideas as starting points, you should be OK.

Musical models are also helpful if you're having trouble communicating ideas to the people you are working with. Very often, all you'll have to do is play a recording with a snare sound or vocal reverb you like to get understanding from your co-workers. This is lots easier than describing a sound you'd like to hear.

Listen to these recordings on the same system you'll be recording with. The reason for this is that you'll get valuable sonic insight to the overall sound of your track as compared to others. Is your track too bright, too dull? Compare it to other recordings you like to see how your track stands up.

Choosing a Tempo

One of your first decisions will be regarding tempo. If you are working with a sequencer, you can always change tempo later, but even so, it's best to get in the ballpark right from the start, since the parts you create will be influenced by the tempo you've chosen. As I suggested before, a musical model can help you get started. As you listen to various recordings, try reciting the lyric (with the phrasing but without the melody) of the song to the recording you're listening to. If the phrasing you want for the lyric feels rushed or dragged, you'll know what adjustments to make. I usually try to find a tempo that's slightly faster than halfway between "too fast" and "too slow." For example, if 100 beats per minute (bpm) is too slow and 120 bpm is too fast, I'll usually choose 116 to 117 bpm. I have my own personal reason for this. I found that my tendency was to make demos that were a shade too slow. Since I used to select the tempo exactly halfway between too fast and too slow, I made a new habit of bumping the tempo up from the midway point. You'll need to find your own personal routine for selecting the perfect tempo, based on the results you get over a period of time. If you aren't the singer, be sure you check with the person who will be singing to find a comfortable tempo.

Selecting a Key

This is the most common mistake I run across in doing demos. You must select the proper key, or you'll be recording the whole demo over again. Here's how to do it.

First, you have to figure the range of the melody. This is easy — just find the highest and lowest notes of the song. Normally, the range will be around an octave and a fourth. Next, you'll need to ask the singer what her range is: What are her lowest and highest notes? Ideally, the range of the melody can be placed within the singer's range. If the range of the melody exceeds the range of the singer, you have two choices: Either change the melody or find another singer. Changing the melody may not be such a big deal. I've often found that a song with too large a range has a lowest note that can be changed with little or no damage to the song. In fact, you may be helping a song by reducing its range.

If changing the melody doesn't work, you'll have to find another singer. Try to find a singer with a range that is larger than that of the song—this will give you flexibility in selecting the key. If the singer is capable of singing the song in the keys of C, C#, D and D#, choose the key that lets the singer sound best for the particular song. Even though the singer can handle any of these keys, his voice might sound better in the lower range. Also, watch out for the singer's "break point." Let me explain. Most singers sing in "chest" (full) and "head" (a higher tone that comes from the singer's head cavities) voices. Low notes are in chest voice, and the higher notes are in head. The transition from chest to head is the break point. Ideally, the singer should be able to gradually switch from full chest to full head by mixing the two voices. One note is in full chest, the next has a little bit of head, the next has more, and so on until a full head tone is produced. Some singers have mastered this transition— you'll never notice them switching from one voice to the other. Other singers have a tough time at the break point. If the melody of the song is centered around the singer's break, you're in for trouble. Even singers with no audible problems at their break may become worn out by the extra effort caused by singing constantly at the break. The good news is that a half-step key change will usually make all the difference.

Another key consideration is the meaning of the song. If it's a sad song, a lower key might get the sadness across more easily. If the song is about the excitement of being in love, a vocal that's pushed to the limit might be even more exciting.

Structure

Maybe you know about song structure—AABA or Verse/Chorus, etc. Arrangment structure goes a little deeper. How long should the intro be? How long a solo? Should there even be a solo? Should the turnaround after the first chorus be two measures or four? The answers to these questions will give you the structure of your demo. With this in mind, you'll want to listen to your musical models for suggestions. Be sure that you plot out every moment of the song with the goal being to *keep the listener's interest*. As I prepare sequences, I'm constantly trying to listen as if I've never heard the song before and noticing when my mind begins to wander or when things simply don't feel right. Usually, I find that I need to shorten some of the sections, but occasionally I will discover that I feel "unsettled" by a turnaround that falls too short.

It's important to try to imagine what the other instruments will be playing when you're sketching out a structure. When you come across a section that feels too long, make mental notes like, "We'll need a guitar fill there," or "I'll put a sample of an atomic bomb in" — whatever works.

Since I don't read music, I'll usually make some notes about the structure that tell me what I'm up to. Here's an example:

COUNT:	2 bars
INTRO:	4 bars
VERSE 1:	8 bars
PRECHORUS 1:	4 bars
CHORUS 1:	8 bars
TURN 1:	2 bars
VERSE 2:	8 bars
PRECHORUS 2:	4 bars
CHORUS 2:	16 bars
BRIDGE:	4 bars
SOLO:	8 bars
PRECHORUS 3:	2 bars
CHORUS 3:	8 bars
OUTRO:	16 bars (fade starts at bar 1)

The sharp-eyed among you will notice that prechorus 3 is half the length of the other prechoruses. This is an arrangement trick designed to accelerate the pace of the song — the listener hears a familiar section, but it gets to the chorus faster. This leads us to . . .

Arrangement Tricks and Traps

Let's face it: Sometimes you need to spice up an arrangement in order to really put the song across. It helps to have a bag of tricks — techniques to keep the arrangement interesting. There are also some traps to avoid. Here's part of my personal list of tricks and traps — the list is partial because it's always changing. I get my ideas from other songwriters, recordings I listen to and magazine articles, as well as coming up with a few myself.

Trick: Play around with the length of the sections within an arrangement. There's no law that says every verse has to be eight measures long just because verse 1 was. The reason I do this is to keep the arrangement interesting; to keep the listener heading into new territory. As I've already mentioned, I like to shorten sections as the song progresses in order to accelerate the pace.

Trap: Be careful not to use this trick (or any other, for that matter) just to use it. You have to try it and listen to it to see if it will work. Any tricks you use will be more successful if they're there for a reason.

Trick: Modulate! Modulation is changing the key of the song. Normally, there is a pivot chord or chord sequence that signals that a new key is coming, but I like simple modulation—just change keys! This technique is very effective in lots of situations, such as a song that has a similar melody or tonal center in both the verse and the chorus. If the verse is in the key of C, try putting the chorus in the key of D. Another situation might be a verse in the key of C that is fine, leading to a chorus in C with a melody that goes too high. Try putting the chorus in B or Bb. You'll need to do lots of experimentation to find the modulation techniques that work for you. (In one song I recorded, I had the modulation occur at the second chorus. It was totally unexpected, and it really gave a boost to the song at that point. As much as I liked using that particular approach, I haven't used it since.)

I generally try to design a modulation that the listener doesn't notice. He or she will still feel the effect of the modulation—a lift or a drop, depending on whether I'm modulating up or down—without being consciously aware of it. I do this by having the modulation occur during a new section the listener hasn't heard before, such as a bridge, leading into the modulated chorus or solo or whatever.

Trap: Since modulation is one of the most effective arrangement tricks there is, it's also one of the most overused. ("Got so bored I had to modulate . . ."—NRBQ.) Try to avoid the predictable modulation, such as just before the last chorus. This battle-ax is usually combined with a *ritardando* (slowing of the tempo).

Trick: Make similar sections different from each other. If verse 1 has piano, guitar, bass and drums, try dropping the piano and adding an organ for verse 2. If choruses 1 and 2 have two-part backing vocals, try three parts of backup on chorus 3. If there's a sidestick snare playing beats 2 and 4 in verse 1, try using sidestick on beat 2 and a snare with a tambourine on beat 4 during verse 2. Remove the bass from the first line of verse 2.

Trick: Accentuate a powerful word in a lyric with a musical device. This one's another cliche, but if you're careful, it can bring a section of a song to life. For example, in a country song with a lyric like "Daddy never knew how close he was to heaven," you might have a guitar do a chimed harmonic at the word *heaven*. Usually, the best place for this musical device is in verse 2—it's the first major section of a song to repeat. Hopefully, there will be a word that's worth punching up. If you use this trick, make it *subtle*.

Trap: Don't use the same tricks in every arrangement—you'll weaken them. Likewise, the more tricks you use in a song, the less effective any individual one will be. You've got to have your own sense of balance between too much and too little. Listen to those musical models. Of course, some songs and styles of music *require* wretched excess, à la "Bohemian Rhapsody."

Trap: Please don't use a two- or four- (or eight-) bar drum pattern for an entire song!

Trick: Use dynamics to breathe life into a song. (I once asked a musician to play with more dynamics. He responded, "I'm playing as loud as I can. . . .") If you start an arrangement at "10", it has nowhere to go but down (which might not be such a bad idea . . . for the right song). Although *dynamics* generally refers to loudness and softness, you can also consider variations in intensity and timbre as part of the dynamics equation. How busy a part is also has an effect on the dynamics. The point here is to make the song like a ride with ups and downs and turns, rather than a trip on an interstate with no curves.

As I say, this is just a partial list—hopefully you'll come up with zillions of others. Also, just because I say things like, "Don't modulate at the last chorus, especially if you combine it with a ritardando," doesn't mean you shouldn't try it for yourself. There's not a rule I can think of that hasn't been broken by one hit record or another.

SEQUENCING BASICS

The MIDI revolution is over—MIDI is now an established way to make demos and records—even augment live music. There are very few musical situations where MIDI is not useful—if you don't use a sequencer for actually playing parts, you can use it to automate your mixdown.

It would be impossible for me to cover every possible sequencer here. Knowing this, there are still some basic approaches that may be helpful to you no matter which sequencer you use.

Groove

The last ten years or so have seen the development of *rhythm* over melody and harmonic structure. Since the introduction of the first drum machines, rhythm has become the key to making a current demo. Being able to create (or re-create) great grooves is essential for successful demos. Fortunately, groove is not tremendously difficult for anyone to learn—all you need is a good drum machine/sequencer, some current recordings and your ears.

Start by choosing a groove from a recording you like. Listen to the instruments, one at a time, and sequence a basic four- or eight-measure groove, comparing it to the original as you go. I usually start with the easy instruments—kick, snare, hat; this is where the meat of the groove is. It also helps to choose sounds that are as close as you can get to the original sounds—they don't have to be perfect copies. Once you've gotten the basic instruments, you may need to listen carefully in order to fine-tune them. For example, if you are copping a hip-hop groove, you'll likely be running into some swung sixteenth notes from the high-hat. Getting the swing to be just right can be difficult, depending on your machine(s); some drum machines and sequencers have limited swing capabilities. In this case, you'll have to hand-edit a measure or two until it's right, then copy the section to the rest of the pattern. When you swing sixteenth notes, you are simply delaying every second and fourth sixteenth note (one E and UH—delay the *E* and the *UH*) by a small amount. Once you find the swing you want, be sure that you check the kick drum for any sixteenth notes, since they'll need to be swung, too.

Next, start listening for other instruments that are part of the main groove, and add them to your pattern. It may take a little time to hear the exact parts, but give it some time. Before you know it, you'll be able to isolate every clave and djimbe on the thickest tracks. Then you'll be ready to do some *serious* fine-tuning. Here are some groove-related tips you'll find really helpful.

Quantizing Grooves

It's easy to simply leave the quantizing permanently active on your sequencer. This can be OK if you're willing to tweak things later on via editing and delaying instruments, but there is another approach you should try: turn the quantizing *off!* It's a little more difficult to sequence this way, but you can definitely achieve grooves that aren't possible with quantizing. If you prefer, try quantizing just the kick drum (perhaps the snare, too) and nothing else—this will give your groove the basic steadiness you need with the humanity of unquantized parts. If your sequencer has "soft" quantizing, which corrects timing errors by a percentage (instead of 100 percent only, you can select 10, 20, 73 percent, whatever), I strongly urge you to learn to use it. This feature speeds up the process of making humanized grooves. By the way, your sequencer may also have a quantizing feature called "humanize": the idea is that the sequencer will introduce slight "errors" in a part to make it sound more human. (On my sequencer, I can specify the range of error I want to introduce.) While this feature is useful, it's not nearly as hip as soft quantizing, and I certainly use it less often.

Delaying Groove Instruments

If you have a sequencer that allows it, try delaying individual instruments by very small amounts. (By *small*, I mean the smallest time division your sequencer or drum machine will allow—hopefully yours will allow you a subdivision of at least $\frac{1}{96}$ of a quarter note.) It really helps to have the individual instruments on separate sequencer tracks; this makes it much easier to manipulate individual instruments. Try delaying the high-hat first. (I almost *always* delay the hat, no matter what type of music I'm working on.) If delaying by $\frac{1}{96}$ sounds good, try delaying by $\frac{2}{96}$; you're looking for the point where the delay is excessive. Besides, if this technique is new to you, you'll need to listen carefully in order to distinguish between various delay settings. Next, try delaying the snare. You may find situations where several instruments are delayed by different amounts. One note of caution: Have your quantizing worked out *before* you start playing around with delaying tracks.

Bass

In much of modern music, the bass is part of the groove, almost as if it were a rhythm instrument. (You can hear the precedent to this approach in the old rock-and-roll and r&b records of the fifties and sixties, where the bass player almost always played the same rhythmic pattern as the kick drum.) So, a good place to start when sequencing the bass is to copy the rhythm of the kick drum part. You don't need to exactly copy the rhythm of the kick—an extra beat here or one fewer there is perfectly OK. The next thing to consider is the rhythm of the lead vocal. To do this, sing (or speak) the lead vocal as you listen to the bass part. If you notice a section that sounds like there's a fight going on, you've found a spot where a change in the rhythm of the bass (and possibly the kick drum) would help. Experiment with a few different approaches until you find one that pleases you. You can also try having the bass do something special while the vocal pauses between lines, or as the song goes from the verse to the chorus, almost like a rhythm fill. When you do fills from one instrument or another, be sure to have all of the other instruments cooperate by not interfering with the fill.

Sometimes, the bass has nothing to do with the kick drum (other than being in time with each other — sometimes not even that), so feel free to try other approaches. For example, the Police song "Every Breath You Take" has a bass part playing constant eighth notes — ONE AND TWO AND THREE AND FOUR AND while the kick plays ONE (two) AND THREE (four) AND. Those of you who are using samplers to make loops from pre-existing recordings may end up with bass parts that technically shouldn't work, but that sound cool anyway. Let your heart be the judge.

If you're having problems knowing which notes to play, start by simply alternating between the root and the fifth of the chord you're on. If the chord is an E, then you can use E (root) and B (fifth) as bass notes. With an A chord, the bass can play A (root) and E (fifth). Get the idea? The next step might be to look for notes that "walk" toward the next chord in the song, such as playing *E, F#, G#, A* as the chords change from E to A. Now, these techniques will get you creating bass parts that are — boring. The ultimate approach is to find a bass part that is a separate melody of its own; just be sure that you don't overdo it and make the bass part too distracting. Ultimately, each part must serve the overall piece of music.

Obviously, it will help your bass chops to listen to other tracks for ideas. When you hear an exceptional bass (or any other instrumental) part, learn how to play or sequence it. The skills you develop this way will serve you many times over in the future.

Piano Keyboard

Once you've got your groove happening (including bass), it's time for the piano or other main keyboard. Now, I've got to tell you that I am one of the world's worst keyboard players, but I'm burnin' on the computer. I end up sequencing the piano a measure or two at a time, editing as I go. If you have the patience, this is a fine way to work. Even so, there are situations that I simply can't cover this way, such as with a song that requires real piano playing. In this case, I hire a real pianist to come over and whip out the part in an hour or two. Here are some tips that will help you do the same:

Hire the Right Player

This tip will make the session much easier for everyone involved. If you need a New Orleans/Dr. John style piano part, *don't* hire the guy who plays like Elton John. Likewise, if you need some cool modern synth parts à la Depeche Mode, *don't* call the guy who's the happening blues player in town.

Don't Quantize Immediately

If the player is really good (which is why you hired her), she will likely play things that hard quantizing would ruin. Often, pianists will slightly "spread" the notes in a chord. This makes the part sound more "pianistic" (piano + realistic = pianistic . . .). If you quantize a spread chord, the result will be lifeless. The best way to handle this situation is to record without quantizing, save the unquantized part, then begin fixing parts that are out of time (or that simply sound bad) with editing and quantizing. Once you've started making changes, save the part/song *WITH A NEW NAME* so that the original unquantized part can always be retrieved. For example, the original song with the unquantized part might be saved as *MYSONG*. Once you start editing, save the song as *MYSONG2*.

Use Soft Quantizing

If your sequencer has "soft" quantizing, learn to use it. Editing a piano part with lots of pianistics can be very time consuming—using soft quantize will speed the process dramatically. (Soft quantize lets you specify how much time correction the sequencer should apply, from 100 percent—full "hard" quantize—to 0 percent—no quantize at all. I often use either 50 percent or 75 percent soft quantize. Some sequencers also let you set a "tolerance" factor, which means that notes that are slightly early or late—you get to set the tolerance to your taste—are not affected by quantizing, soft or hard.)

Use the Highest Resolution Your Sequencer Allows

Resolution is the amount of subdivisions your sequencer allows per quarter note. The standard for stand-alone sequencers is 96 pulses per quarter note (ppq), but this is not nearly enough resolution for piano. My sequencer has double this resolution (192 ppq) and it is barely tolerable. I've had too many situations where the pianist played something that the sequencer changed ever so slightly, never for the better. Oh well. You do the best you can with what you've got. . . .

Emotional Sequencing

Emotional sequencing is an oxymoron if I've ever heard one, like *military intelligence* or *fat-free ham*. How can you possibly get emotion into a computer?

The answer is simple—*you* have to put it there when you play. When you play a bass part, get involved and really perform it. When you sequence the drums, pretend you're a drummer and play the way you feel. If you are operating the computer while someone else plays, help him get into the part by grooving along with him, just as if he were recording onto tape. The result will be performances that have much more life to them.

By the way, one sure way to kill the emotion in a sequence is to set all the velocities the same on every part. There are exceptions— times when you want the drums to be robotic and mindlessly obnoxious—but overall, those slight imperfections of velocity (and timing) provide the human element that can make all the difference.

MIDI Controllers

There's a whole category of MIDI information that you can use to supercharge your studio. These are MIDI controllers; they are numbered from 0 to 127, and most of them allow values from 0 to 127. Some of these numbers are assigned to certain functions: for example, #1 is assigned to mod. wheel, #7 is assigned to MIDI volume, #64 is assigned to sustain. By the way, since sustain is either "on" or "off", the normal values used are 0 (for "off") and 127 (for "on").

The fun starts when you apply these controllers to your effects devices. Most modern effects boxes let you assign a MIDI controller to a parameter—in fact, most let you assign two or more controllers to a patch. Let's say that you want the vocal reverb to get quieter during a section of the song. Look in the manual for the effects device you'll be using and find out how to assign a controller to "reverb level" or "master level." Once you've done this, use your sequencer to record the moves you want to make. This can get a little tricky, since you'll have to figure out how to get your master keyboard to transmit the controller you've chosen; some master keyboards let you assign a fader to a controller, and others let you use a pedal. If you can't get this to happen, you can always insert the controller directly into your sequencer in "edit" mode. You'll have to be sure to match MIDI channels with the sequencer track and the device, and you'll also want to avoid using the same channel as another instrument, since you may cause some unwanted interferences.

This process of learning how to get your sequencer talking to your effects devices may take you an entire weekend, so don't worry if you initially have some trouble getting it to happen. There are so many different sequencers and so many different effects devices that it would take several books to explain all the possibilities, but take heart! Within your circle of friends and acquaintances is someone who can help. I have a network of folks I call with MIDI questions, and there are plenty of times when they call me for help. Look for those local experts and *study your manuals*!

The Dummy Demo

If you have your own studio, even if it's fairly modest, one of the best things you can do is to make a *dummy demo* — a quick, uncritical, fun, first whack at the song you're working on. Dummy demos are not meant to be heard by the general public; they're for you to work out parts, to try out a vocal approach or an arrangement. The key to a great dummy demo is not to agonize over anything. Don't think about it — *do it*! A dummy demo should take you as little as an hour to do, and no more than an evening. If you spend longer, you've spent too much time.

I probably shouldn't tell you this (you'd find out on your own), but if you've got some pretty good equipment, and you've developed the habit of recording good, clean tracks, your dummy demo can occasionally evolve into a final. That's because the unguarded performances that the dummy demo encourages are very often superior to performances you sweat over. Just be sure to keep the pressure off the process. Have fun, take chances, try out some ideas. The point here is to come up with a tape you'll listen to later so that you can make those arrangement decisions before you do the real demo.

TIME CODE

In order to lock your computer to your multitrack machine, you'll need to use a time code or sync track. The idea is that by printing time code on one track of your multitrack, you'll be able to have your computer ignore its own built-in time reference (clock) and follow the tape machine. Your MIDI tracks will play at a tempo based on the tape machine's sync track, and you'll be able to record live instruments and vocals that are synced to the computer.

Types of Time Code

There are several types of sync. The first, and most basic, is frequency shift key (FSK). This type of sync is used for most drum machines and inexpensive stand-alone sequencers, and it has a few major drawbacks. First, FSK does not allow the computer to "chase" the tape machine—you must always start the tape at the beginning of the song, even if all you want to hear is the last chorus. There is a version of FSK called Smart FSK that does allow chasing, but the other drawback of FSK remains: The tempo of your song is locked to the tempo written into FSK. If you should decide that your song needs to be just a bit faster, you'll have to restripe the tape with FSK written with a faster tempo.

The preferred type of sync is Society of Motion Picture and Television Engineers (SMPTE) since it allows chasing and the ability to change tempo without restriping. There are four types of SMPTE, referenced to four types of film/video standards, and the four types are not compatible. You cannot stripe your tape with one type and try to "read" it as another. The four types of SMPTE are 24 (film), 25 (European video standard—color and black-and-white), 30 drop (American color video) and 30 non-drop (American black-and-white video), and the numbers refer to the various frame rates. Unless you are syncing to picture, you should probably use 30 non-drop SMPTE code, since it is more or less a standard for music-only applications. Your sequencer/computer setup may be different, so check out the owner's manual before you make any permanent decisions. If you will be syncing to picture, you'll have to use the appropriate frame rate for the format you'll be using.

SMPTE code is written as absolute time—hours, minutes, seconds and frames (this is where the different types of SMPTE show up). You can set a start time from your sequencer that corresponds to a particular point on your tape; for example, 00 hours, 05 minutes, 10 seconds and 27 frames. Normally, you'll want to use a more "even" start time, such as 00 hours, 05 minutes, but the point is that you can start at any single frame within any second. This will come in handy in some situations.

Time Code Technique

Here are some ways to get the most out of using time code.

Use SMPTE Time Code

Yes, I know I've already said it, but this point is so important that it bears repeating.

Stripe the Whole Tape at Once

Since you'll be able to start chasing SMPTE anywhere on the tape, it will save you time if you simply stripe your tape before you first use it; the next time you start working, this chore will already be done.

Use an Outside Track for Time Code

Unless you're using a machine with a dedicated time code track, use an outside track (either track 1 or 16 on a 16-track machine, track 1 or 8 on an 8-track) for time code. The reason is that the sound of the time code will "leak" from its own track to any adjacent tracks. Outside tracks have only one adjacent track.

Print a Hot-Enough Signal

Most time code problems result from not printing a hot enough time code signal on tape. You should first try printing code directly from your MIDI interface or other time code source. If the level that shows up on your tape machine meter is close to -5 dB (5 dB less than 0 dB), you'll probably have enough level, although some experimentation will be necessary. If you experience problems, such as having your sequencer stop unexpectedly while chasing time code, try printing with a hotter level. Take the output of your time code source, and run it into the line input of one of your mixer channels. Take the direct out or the "send" portion of the "insert" of this channel and run it into the appropriate channel on your multitrack recorder. You'll now be able to add gain to the time code, but be careful! Be sure to set the line trim and fader properly (review the mixer section of this book if you need to know how to do this) to avoid distortion or noise, and *be sure you don't use any eq*! Once again, experiment to determine if the level you are using is going to work. On occasion, I have had to print a very hot signal: +6 dB. If you still have difficulties, the problem may be elsewhere—for example, in your computer software or your MIDI interface. If you need to, call the software and MIDI interface company and ask for technical support.

In some situations, like when nothing else works, a time code "refresher" will be called for. This is a small box with an input and an output, a level control, and some indicator lights. This device receives SMPTE time code at its input and puts out brand new, "refreshed" SMPTE at its output. The level control lets you set the gain of the SMPTE to a level that your sync box or MIDI interface wants to see.

Don't Use Noise Reduction on the Time Code Track

Most multitrack recorders allow you to defeat (turn off) the noise reduction on an individual track. This is so that the noise reduction circuitry won't mess up the time code signal. If you're printing code fairly hot and using Dolby noise reduction, this precaution may not be necessary, since Dolby is essentially "off" at O dB. DBX noise reduction is always on, so it *must* be turned off to avoid time code problems.

Allow a Little Bit of Start Time at the Top

Let's say you started striping your tape with a SMPTE time of 00 hours, 00 minutes, 00 seconds and 00 frames. Start your first song at 10 seconds at the very soonest, to allow any computers or drum machines some "reading time." If you don't do this, you will experience odd starting tempos and other problems. For film and video work, it's common to use much longer amounts of code before the start time in order to allow lots of flexibility when the music is finally dubbed onto the videotape or film. Also, if there is the possibility of needing to sync additional tape machines (audio or video) via SMPTE, you'll want to have an even longer space before the start time, since multiple machines may require a longer "lockup" time — 10 seconds of lockup is not unheard of.

Yet another potential problem for some machines is starting SMPTE at 00 hours, 00 minutes, 00 seconds and 00 frames. These machines may misbehave each time they are forced to "read" this time; in this case, simply start striping at a later time, such as 01 hours, 00 minutes, 00 seconds and 00 frames.

If You Experience a "Dropout"

If your time code track develops a *dropout* — a spot on the tape that loses the signal you recorded — you've got some real problems. You'll know you have a dropout because the machines that are synced to the time code will either "hiccup" or stop altogether. You can try cleaning the heads or running the time code coming off the tape through something that will increase the gain, but chances are you'll have to do some major surgery. If you're using FSK, the code that has tempo info locked into it, you could have even more severe problems if the machine that "wrote" the original code is no longer available. For example, say you wrote the code when you first started working on the song. It's now six months later (maybe you've changed the lyrics . . . ?) and you've recently upgraded your computer to a newer model. Chances are very good that the new computer has a slightly different idea of what 120 bpm is compared to the old computer. Why does this matter? The reason is that unless cleaning the heads or increasing the gain worked, you're going to have to *re-record the time code*, and new time code from a new machine may not match the old. (In this case, you may have to adjust certain sections of your sequence.) "What???!!!" you say — "How will I ever get the starting point of the new code to line up with the tracks I made based on the old code?" Guess what: There's no need to get the new code's starting point to match the old code's start. All you have to do is make sure that the new code's start point is *before* the old start point, within a second or so. You can then adjust your sequence's start beat until it's close. If your music started on sequence beat 9 (you always allow a count-in measure or two, don't you?), you may have to "move" the entire piece of music within the sequence so that the first beat of music occurs later, say on beat 13, or perhaps the last sixteenth note of beat 13. Get the starting beat as close as you can with these adjustments. Once you're really close, connect the time code tape track's output to a digital delay, and the delay's output back into the computer's time code input. You can now adjust the time code in very small increments until your computer "locks" to the previously recorded tracks. By the way, if your FSK code has time changes in it — *accelerando* or *ritardando* — you may just want to re-record the whole song! (Actually, if I were in that situation, I'd keep trying to get the start time of the new code as close as I could to the old start location in hopes that the tempo changes would be close enough to the already-recorded tracks.)

This points out the beauty of SMPTE. Since SMPTE code has no tempo information in it, you can simply re-record the code and keep moving the start time of your sequence until it's right. Once you've gotten to the point that the right start time is in between single frames (00 hours, 00 minutes, 05 seconds and 12 frames is too soon, and 00 hours, 00 minutes, 05 seconds and 13 frames is too late), connect up the digital delay and adjust until it's perfect. All of your tempo changes should line up perfectly.

That's about all there is to it, especially with music-only work. For your first few experiences with a film- or video-related project, you might want to arrange to have some help from someone experienced in the format you'll be using. They'll be able to help you to handle the particulars of the project you're working on.

NOISE

Noise is your enemy, when it comes to making great demos. Where does noise come from? The primary sources are acoustic and electrical, and you need to learn how to deal with each. First, the bad news — noise always occurs and it will always be there hiding in your tracks. The good news is that with a little work (and trickery), you can reduce the level of noise to a point that it won't interfere with your music.

Let's start with acoustic noise — noise that occurs more or less naturally. I'm talking about cars passing on the street, air conditioning, the TV playing in the next room, rainstorms, etc. This type of sonic interference is a fact of life. You won't be able to keep it from occurring, although you might be able to limit the amount that gets into your studio.

Choose Your Studio Location Carefully

If you are starting from scratch, possibly even getting ready to lease some space, you can just as easily choose a naturally quiet location as a noisy one. Listen for traffic noise, plumbing sounds and air conditioning, and check out your potential neighbors. Even if they are noisy, perhaps it will be for only a few hours a day, leaving the rest of the day for you.

If you're like the rest of us, your studio will by necessity be located somewhere in your living space. There are lots of things to consider: How much room do you really need? Is there a closet (a potential isolation booth) in the room? Is the room fairly secure? (Thieves love musical gear.) Are there enough electrical outlets? What kind of noise will be coming from the surrounding rooms? (Hopefully, you've got a cooperative roommate or spouse.)

Block Out Outside Noise

It's important to be able to close doors and windows when you need a quiet work environment. You may also need to kill the air conditioning to quiet your room down. Even if the temperature is going to be very uncomfortable while you record, the lower noise level will make a major difference in your tracks.

Deaden Your Room

When noise hits a flat, reflective surface, like glass or plaster, it bounces. Multiple reflective surfaces mean multiple bounces, and with each bounce, the sound changes. If the reflective surfaces are parallel, the reflections are more efficient—bad for noise control. If your room is "noisy," meaning live and reflective, you'll get lots of unwanted sonic reflections recorded along with the sounds you want to record. For these reasons, it's best to try to deaden your room with nonreflective material. You can use blankets, but you'll soon find that it can be difficult to hang the blankets so that they won't fall down, not to mention that the blankets won't work as well as other materials. The best material to use is acoustic foam, which is designed to absorb as much sound as possible. There are very expensive and very cheap versions; the more expensive stuff works a little better and lasts a lot longer, and the cheap stuff can dry rot within five years or so. In most instances, the cheap stuff will do fine.

Make an Iso Booth or Corner

Recording a vocal usually requires a very quiet environment—you want to record only the singer's voice, not the reflections from nearby walls or windows. In "real" studios, an isolation booth is used to minimize outside sounds and inside reflections. You can do the same at your house. One approach is to use a large closet, a bathroom, a hallway or another room in the house as the iso booth. If the room you use is quite large and naturally dead, you *might* get by without using sound deadening material on the walls, but in most cases, you'll need to dampen the room. With a large closet, this is no problem — just put up some more acoustic foam and you're done. With other rooms, it's another story entirely. Unless you have a very understanding (or unaware) roommate or spouse, you'll have to make some compromises. Maybe you can find a way to make the foam easily removable for those times when the room is used for normal life.

The second alternative is to make an iso corner in your studio. Unless you've already covered every square inch of wall and ceiling with foam, you can simply choose one corner to be used for vocals, and deaden it to the max. The singer can then either face into the corner or out into the room. If you've done a good job, the room reflections that make it back to the mic should be minimal.

Get Rid of Noise Inside Your Room

Your room will almost certainly have some noises in it that you can minimize. A big one for me is computer noise. Most computers have fans inside them to keep them cool. If you defeat the fan, you'll really quiet down your room, but *your computer will die*, so this isn't really a workable solution. Try moving the CPU (central processing unit — the box part of the computer) to a location that's quieter, perhaps behind some other piece of gear. You may need to buy extension cables for your keyboard and monitor, but the small investment will be worth it. Be sure not to endanger your computer's CPU by putting it in a dusty location or in a spot where lots of direct sunlight will hit it. Also, be sure that you'll be able to reach the CPU for those times when you need to install or remove a disk.

Other pieces of gear, such as power amps, have fans in them, too, so you'll have to use similar tactics in order to minimize their interference. One of my guitar amps has a fan in it, and I am able to defeat it (I simply unplugged the cable going to it), since I generally don't use the amp at full volume or for very long periods of time. If you've got an amp with a fan, you might try the same thing, but do so at your own risk!

Electrical noise is a whole other animal, and avoiding it is just as important as avoiding acoustic noise. Here are some procedures to help.

Set Your Studio Up Properly

Every few years, I tear my studio down and start all over. There are several jobs that can be accomplished only this way. The first is the elimination of dust and dirt that has built up over time. Next is "rearranging the furniture"—moving the location of various items in the attempt to make my studio easier to work in. Lastly, I get to rewire the whole dang thing.

There's a big advantage to rewiring. See, if your studio is at all like mine, you add equipment one or two pieces at a time. After a few years, you've hooked up almost a dozen new pieces, and they may not have been connected with the whole studio in mind. Starting over allows you to fix this situation.

Once you've torn everything down (hah!), begin hooking everything back up, starting with the power amp and studio monitors. Connect the studio monitors to the power amp, and plug the power amp (but *nothing else*) into an AC source. (If you have a power conditioner, all the better.) With no input plugged into the power amp, you should hear virtually no noise when the power amp is on and the levels are set to maximum. If you hear hum, you've already got a problem. The possibilities are few at this point, since there are very few variables. These possibilities are 1) the power amp is faulty; 2) the line current is faulty; or 3) the grounding is faulty (this is really a variation of #2). If you've never had problems with the power amp before, it's probably the grounding, or possibly the line current itself. For grounding problems you can try lifting the ground with a ground-lifting adapter (available at a hardware store near you—these very useful adapters will also allow you to try reversing the polarity of a three-prong AC plug). As you may have guessed from the previous parenthetical phrase, the next trick to try is reversing the polarity of the AC plug. Between the variables of grounded/ground lifted and polarity normal/polarity reversed, you will find the quietest way to plug in the power amp. If they all sound the same, go for grounded with normal polarity. (If you know how to do it, or if you know an electrician, you might check the outlets in your house to make sure they've been wired properly. I've also seen gizmos that plug into a three-prong AC socket and check the wiring for you; you should be able to find one of these at an electrical supply company for a few dollars.)

If you still hear hum after trying ground lifting and phase reversal, you may need a line conditioner (a devise that "cleans" AC—you plug it into the wall and then plug your studio into it) or repairs on your power amp. If your power amp is up and running quietly, move on to the next step.

Next up is your mixer. Before you plug anything in, turn your power amp off to avoid unpleasant noises that could threaten your monitors. Hook the main mixer outputs to the power amp inputs, and the mixer to AC power. Be sure that all faders and output controls on the mixer are at minimum. Turn the mixer on first, then the power amp, and listen for hum and noise. You can now try lifting the ground and/or reversing the AC polarity on the mixer— be sure to turn the power amp off before you unplug the mixer's AC. Once again, you should be able to find the quietest orientation of the mixer's AC cable.

By now you should be getting the idea. When you have the mixer set up, proceed to your multitrack machine, hooking up input and output cables and power. Once again, be sure to turn your power amp off while you're connecting cables and orienting AC plugs.

So far, you should have had no trouble at all getting everything quiet—no hum whatsoever. The final phase of connections is where most of your problems will come from: the effects. Just as you hooked up the mixer and multitrack machine separately, you must also connect up each effect device, one at a time. It's a pain, but it will let you find any problems easily. So, connect up each effect device, one at a time—inputs, outputs and AC—and adjust for minimum hum-ness. By the way, you should set each effect to "dry" only—no effect—since some effects make noise by their nature. Also, many effects nowadays are powered by separate power supplies, affectionately referred to as "wall warts." These power supplies and their cables send off electromagnetic fields that may be picked up by other wiring, causing (you guessed it) hum. If the hum changes when you move the wall wart, you've found the culprit; just move it to a noninterfering location.

If all of the effects are in a rack, you can start with all of them physically installed. Most racks, by their very nature, set up a common chassis ground for everything installed in them, since each device is attached to metal (electrically conductive) rack rails with metal screws. Common grounding is usually an advantage, although there may be one piece of equipment that needs to be isolated from the others in the rack. If you have a piece of gear that you cannot silence by normal means, try removing it from the rack, breaking the chassis ground. If this works, you can get some special rack screws and nonconductive washers to install this piece — you'll probably also need to leave space above and below the isolated piece, so that it doesn't physically touch any other devices.

Occasionally, you'll try everything to no avail. Your studio is hum-free, until you plug in this one piece; then all hell breaks loose. Even though you've found the best orientation for the AC and tried isolating the chassis from the other devices, you still get noticeable hum. The reason is that there is a ground loop from your input and output cables. You'll need to isolate one or the other of them. Here's how to isolate an input cable: Start with a spare cable of the appropriate type. At the end that will be connected to the mixer, disconnect the shield (the braided metal layer just underneath the outer insulation). You can accomplish this in two ways, either by desoldering the shield inside the jack, or, if the jack itself is sealed, by peeling away about ½ inch of insulation close to the jack and carefully cutting the braided shield all the way around. When you're done, use colored electrician's tape to both cover up your surgery and mark the cable. This way, you'll know that the shield has been cut. Try this cable on the input, and use regular cables on the output. Notice that you need to isolate only the input or the output, not both. Breaking one shield will break the ground loop.

Cable Hygiene

Use good cable (go to a reputable music store and ask for suggestions). The cheap stuff will cause noise and breakdowns, and generally make your life miserable. Also, when you are laying out cable, be sure you don't run audio cable near AC lines — the audio cable will pick up noise from the AC. If audio cable must run near AC lines, be sure to lay the audio across the AC at a perpendicular angle rather than running the cables alongside each other in parallel. Also, try to avoid making coils of cable; coiled AC cable can set up an electromagnetic field, and coiled audio cable seems to attract noise.

Learn to Set Levels

Setting levels is one of the easiest ways to make or break your demos. If you don't pay attention and set levels improperly to effects, tape machines, inputs, etc., you'll get noise and distortion, both of which are entirely unnecessary. Levels must be set high enough to avoid the inherent noise in every device, and low enough to avoid overload distortion. The meters on your effects make it easy to see when overloading is occurring; remembering to see if you've got the level set high enough (in order to avoid noise) is another thing entirely. Get in the habit of setting effects inputs as high as possible without overloading. If you aren't sure if the levels are set high enough, you can solo the device in question and purposely set the level too high in order to hear what this particular box's distortion sounds like. You can then back the level down until the distortion disappears. This is a good way to get familiar with the capabilities of each of your effects (and other) devices, since they will each behave quite differently. Some distort at the slightest flicker of an overload indicator; others have more room to give once the overload light comes on. By the way, you can get by with effects levels that are set improperly during tracking, as long as you aren't printing the effects. At mix time, it's critical that you get the levels right, although levels don't have to be perfect until the mix is actually being run.

Multi-effects boxes have more-than-simple input and output levels to set. There are internal level settings for each effect in the multi-effect chain — improper settings will cause noise or distortion problems. Also, multi-effects generally seem to be especially touchy about overload distortion; they go from clean to overloaded with very little transition. If you hear distortion from a multi-effect, and the input levels look cool, try backing them down just a shade.

Noise Reduction

There are occasions when the signal you want to record is noisy by its nature, such as a very distorted guitar, or an older keyboard instrument. In these cases, it's a great help to have a single-ended noise reduction unit, which works on any sound. This type of unit works much like a frequency sensitive noise gate, letting sounds through once they cross a user-selected threshold. Noise gates block all frequencies or let them all through. The single-ended noise reduction units are more sophisticated, dividing the sound into multiple frequency bands and adjusting the levels of each frequency band rather than simply turning them on and off. If you send in a noisy bass guitar signal, the single-ended noise reduction unit would let bass frequencies and some midfrequencies through while blocking the high-mids and the high frequencies—depending on how well you set the threshold. There are a few manufacturers of these rack mount boxes, such as Roland and Rocktron, and they are priced over a wide range, from around $200 to more than $1,000. By the way, the noise reduction unit I use was quite inexpensive—I bought it used for $125 . (Tape-recorder-based noise reduction systems are double-ended, since they process the sound before it is recorded onto the tape, and also when the taped sound is played. This type of noise reduction is meant to reduce tape hiss, and it will not work in any other fashion.)

Recording Clean Tracks

There's lots to be gained (that is, noise to be avoided) by careful use of your tape machine at track time. If the part you're recording runs from top to bottom of your song, it's no problem; just start recording. In the case of a vocal or other part that starts and stops all the way through the song, you can avoid noise buildup by going out of record during the quiet sections. It helps if you know the song—even so, watch the singer/performer like a hawk—he will give you visual cues as to when to re-enter record. (I watch for breath intake, which lets me know that singing is imminent.)

It's helpful to be recording on a track that's already clean—no old parts or portions still on the track. If you're sure the track is clean, great. If not, listen down and make sure. If you need to erase, make sure that you're really prepared to lose what's on the track. Once you're sure, record over the track *with nothing plugged into the input of the tape machine.* This will ensure that no sound is recorded.

Cleaning Recorded Tracks

Sometimes, you have no choice but to record tracks with un- wanted noise on them. If the noise occurs during sounds you want to keep, you'll have to live with it, or re-record. If the noise occurs in the spaces between the keeper parts, you can try cleaning the noise by recording over the noisy places on the tape with no input. You'll need to have nerves of steel, since a mistake will cost you the loss of a keeper part. If your machine has automated punch-out (or auto stop), you can use this feature to make sure that you don't erase any further than you want, but be careful; depending on your tape machine, the auto punch-out feature may or may not be accurate enough to do the job you have in mind. If your machine's tape counter "drifts" too much, you may accidentally erase parts you need to keep.

Setting the punch-out location is critical. When the punch-out location is very close (within a fraction of a second) to the re-entry of the keeper part, you can use a few tricks to minimize danger. First: Rehearse the punch-out, automated or manual, until you're sure it will work. Second: Remember that it's better to erase too little than to erase too much—you can always try again if you don't clean all the noise. Third: Use your tape machine's pitch control to slow the tape speed. This will make it easier for you to punch out in time if you're working manually, and if you're doing an auto punch-out, the reduced tape speed will mean that the punch-out occurs over a shorter distance of tape. Fourth: For those willing to live dangerously, you can set the auto-punch location very tightly by marking the place on the tape where you want to punch out with a china marker. You'll need to defeat the tape lifters on your machine (if your machine allows you to do it—most do) so that you hear sound when you move the reels by hand (this is called "rocking" the reels). Be sure you know which tape head you're listening to—if you don't know, *stop* and read the section on tape machines before continuing. By rocking the reels while soloing the track you need to clean, you'll be able to find the absolute latest point to punch out. Mark the tape at this point with the china marker. Now, move the marked location from the playback head to a position *before* the erase head, and then a few inches farther. Set the auto punch-out. Next, rewind the tape and rehearse the punch-out, noticing where the mark on your tape ends up. If the tape has stopped before the marker passes the erase head, you're fine to go ahead and erase. On some machines, it may even be OK if the mark moves past the erase head, since the punch-out may have already occurred before the machine was able to stop. Remember that your machine will act differently from any other machine, so you'll have to experiment to perfect this procedure.

Electromagnetic Fields

Your studio is likely to have many built-in noise makers. A common problem is clock (and other) noise from microprocessors, which is transmitted into the air much like a radio broadcast for

unsuspecting audio devices to pick up. (Similar problems have occurred on airline flights; laptop computers and CD players are
blamed for radar and communications-gear interference.) Nowadays, studios have dozens of microprocessors, from the tape machine to the remote control to the digital reverbs and effects to the
MIDI keyboards to the guitar synth to the MIDI drum pads. Each
of these pieces has a microprocessor inside, ready to add noise to
your system. Another problem (already mentioned) is the wall wart
style of power supplies, found on many effects and drum machines.
(Additionally, the way your cables are run makes a difference—see:
"Cable Hygiene" on page 100). Here are some steps to follow.

When you find a noise, try to isolate it by turning things off, one
at a time. When the noise disappears, you've found your noise
maker. (With pieces using wall wart power supplies, you may need
to unplug the power supply rather than simply turn the device off,
since the power supply operates as long as it's plugged in.) Once
you've found the offending piece, try moving the cables connected
to the device to see if the noise changes, either louder or softer. If
this works, you can find the optimum location for the cables involved. If it doesn't, try physically moving the device to a new location, holding it in your hand and moving it around to see if the
noise changes. Once again, this will tell you where to locate the
piece.

Grounding Ghosts

I have had the very frustrating experience of a "floating" ground
loop: When I would first start up my studio, everything was fine
for an hour or so, then suddenly, without warning, my studio would
develop a serious grounding *"hummmmm."* The only cure turned
out to be to turn the entire studio off, then on again. Things would
be silent for another hour, then, like magic, the noise would recur.
I never found the cause, and it disappeared forever a few weeks
later. (My theory is that there were some problems in the AC line,
so maybe a line conditioner would have helped.) If you get a situation like this, try the restart procedure I've described; you may not
be able to permanently cure the problem, but at least you'll be able
to get some work done!

Step Two

TRACKING

BUILDING TRACKS

OK—You've gone through all the preparation needed to start your song. The next step is to record the tracks, usually piece by piece, until you have all the pieces you'll need for a great demo. Just to keep you on your toes, you may notice that I use the words *track* and *tracks* in a rather confusing fashion. That is, when I say *track*, I may be referring to the entire recording (or song), or to just a part of the recording, such as "the lead guitar track." When I say *tracks*, I may be referring to a group of recordings (or songs), or all of the composite bits (lead guitar track, bass track, etc.) that make up a song (or track . . .). This bit of ambiguity aside, we're ready to begin.

As I said, most often you'll be assembling your track (or song) one track (individual instrument—also called a *part*) at a time. The obvious exception to this is if you have a group of musicians ready and able to record your song several parts at once. In the home studio, this is a rarity, since the space required to record several instruments simultaneously is not usually available. Don't let this deter you: Perhaps you have a wonderful and adoring spouse who will let you turn the living room into a drum booth and the kitchen into the guitar-isolation area "for just a few days." (If you are one of these exceptionally fortunate people, congratulations!) The other technical problems you will face are beyond the scope of this book, so you'll want to look elsewhere for tips on miking drums, etc.

Building tracks one part at a time has several advantages. First, you can be very careful about the sounds you're working on, since you're only working on one sound at a time. Second, you can be more picky about the part itself, since you'll be working on it in isolation. Next, hearing the track build one step at a time gives you a much better understanding of how individual parts relate to each other. There are some disadvantages, however. You won't be able to hear the entire arrangement until all the pieces are assembled. This means your imagination will be very important as you try to guess what the whole thing is going to sound like. It's also difficult to remain passionate about performances as you chip away at the little bits that make up a recording. With experience, these disadvantages can at least be compensated for. Each demo you do will make it easier for you to judge the effect of each part you add, and making sure that the performances are passionate is simply a habit to be developed.

Let's look at some concepts that apply to tracking.

Production Prosody

In songwriting, *prosody* refers (among other things) to matching the tone of the lyric with the melody. For example, in a song with the phrase "I feel happy," you would probably find a melody that rose in pitch, while the lyric "I feel sad" would probably be mated to a descending melody. In constructing a track, I try to use production values and instrument selection to further strengthen the tone or mood of the song. If the song is about how lonely and sad the singer is, I might use a very small room type of reverb or even no reverb at all. If the song is about the civil war in Bosnia, I might use artillery sounds as drums. I don't want to give you too many examples here, because this technique will work best if you take the time to really consider what the song is about and then make sonic decisions that reflect *your* feelings.

Ramping Up

When you listen to a song, do you prefer a song that starts at one level of intensity and then stays there for three and a half minutes, or do you prefer to be taken on a ride, with shifting levels of intensity? I prefer the ride, and I usually prefer the ride to get more interesting or intense as it progresses. That is what I mean by *ramping up*. The idea is to maintain the listener's interest from the moment the song begins until it ends. The *outro* (after the last full chorus, when the song starts repeating a simplified version of the chorus or verse) is one of the best places to start considering as you begin this process, since all too often the outro is simply a repetition of what has already been heard. (I can't tell you how many times I've seen a publisher or producer turn off a tape once the predictable outro has arrived.) This is why I almost always try to do something special as the outro begins. I add a new instrument, I modulate, I put in a pause, I change the lyric — anything to make the outro a new section of the song.

As I've already mentioned in "Arrangement Tricks and Traps," dynamics play an important role in maintaining the listener's interest. Keep this in mind as you build your track, and consider the dynamics of each instrument you record. They don't all have to match — perhaps the drums will suddenly get quiet and then quickly build back up as the guitar starts a screaming solo at full volume. Besides volume, you can apply the concept of dynamics to the density of the arrangement (how many instruments are playing at once as well as how complex the part itself is); tempo (try taking the speed up a touch at the choruses, or using a ritard just before the final chorus — there are unlimited variations on this sort of thing); emotional intensity of the parts; etc.

While the overall effect of the track should be to build from the intro through the outro, there will be moments in a track when intensity should drop, even if only for a moment. This gives the listener a break, a chance to catch her breath. Your first verse might be sparse, a prechorus might add some instruments and complexity, and the first chorus would build further into the first real high point of the song. Next, you could have a brief turnaround that drops the intensity a bit, leading into the even lower-intensity second verse. (Usually the second verse will be more intense than the first verse, the second pre more intense than the first pre, etc.) These are not hard-and-fast rules: For example, you could have the turnaround drop to almost nothing, in which case going into the second verse would be a lift. The test is to *listen to your track as if you've never heard it before* and to notice when you get bored. This is easier than you might think; just *pretend* to be the VP of A&R in LA (or NY) at a major label (MCA, A&M, BMG, WEA?) when you listen to the song!

The House of Cards

Here's a very simple and useful technique that you can use at almost any stage of making your demo. If you compare your song to a house of cards, you can try "pulling out" various cards (elements) one at a time, then evaluating the results. As long as you like the results, you can keep pulling cards. Once the house of cards falls, simply replace the last element you removed. This technique encourages simplicity, or better yet, elegance, which is one of the most difficult things to achieve in anything. It also requires that you listen *in context* — with the other parts playing.

Timbre Wars

Most of us have favorite sounds that we use again and again. Overall, this is a good thing — some repetition of sound from song to song helps to give your work "conceptual continuity," to quote the late Frank Zappa. You also cannot be unique unless you have definite personal preferences.

One thing to watch for is when your favorite sounds compete with each other, or when your one most favorite sound takes up so much sonic space that there's no room for anything else — like vocals. Modern synths are capable of extremely complex sounds, and it's all too easy to let them take over. For example, one songwriter I work with loves a particular M1 patch that sounds like a string pad (a *pad* is a long, slow sound with very little attack — bite — and lots of sustain) mixed with gurgling water, all heavily doused with the M1's built-in reverb and chorus. He uses this patch on almost every one of his songs. When he bought another synth to add to his collection, he chose one with — take a guess — more watery sounds. Stacking these new watery sounds with the old ones resulted in a really murky soundscape. This situation is curable — starting with reducing the amount of effects on the patches. Next, try simplifying the parts, such as eliminating notes that are octaves of each other. (This is a variation of the house of cards technique.) Your track will be noticeably clearer. If it's still not clear enough, you need to change at least one of the offending sounds. You've just become a casualty of the Timbre Wars.

Avoiding this conflict means expanding your sonic palette. If all of your favorite sounds are pads, you need to get involved with sounds that "plunk": pianos, acoustic guitars, tuned percussion. If your favorite sounds are huge and fat, you need to investigate little, thin sounds. On their own they may sound weeny, but in the proper place, they can make your musical point without murdering other, more important, parts. You'll find that you can have more parts (complexity) the more percussive the individual parts are. If you insist on multiple pads, go for smaller, thinner sounds. Small and thin sounds take up a narrower band of frequencies than the big, fat, lush sounds that we all know and love.

Parts and Counterpoint

Well, as we all know, parts is parts. Put the proper parts together and you've got a whole something, be it a symphony or a car. Put a bunch of parts that have no relation to each other together and you've got a mess, or at least something that's a bit confused. Think about this as you build your tracks—your goal is to have parts that help the track, that contribute by their inclusion

One way to develop parts that work together is to use *counterpoint*—parts and melodies that have different rhythms from each other. Say you have a bass part that is playing straight quarter notes—ONE TWO THREE FOUR—every measure. If another instrument is added, playing the same rhythm, the result will be boredom after a few measures. If the new part comes in playing a few eighth notes—(one) AND (two) AND (three) AND (four)—every other measure, the result will be far more interesting for a longer period of time. This is the basic idea, and you'll find that the more you experiment, the more interesting your counterpoint ideas will become. If you're new to this idea, it helps to learn to isolate the melodies or chords you're working with from the rhythm you are using to play them. You can do this by imagining that the instruments playing the parts are really percussion instruments. If you start thinking of the acoustic guitar as a shaker, you'll be able to fine-tune the part to best serve the song.

Dynamics

A common mistake I hear in demos is limited (and sometimes the total lack of) dynamics. The song starts at "11"—and has nowhere to go but down. As you make your tracks, remember the ramping-up concept, and apply it to volume levels. It's usually good to have the dynamics of the song make a shape like a roller coaster: intro–7; verse–5, prechorus–6; chorus–8; turnaround–7; verse 2–6; prechorus 2–7; chorus 2–9; bridge–10; solo–8; out choruses–9. This is just an example, but hopefully you'll get the idea—use dynamics to increase the expressiveness of your track.

On MIDI tracks, you can do this by making sure that the kick is loudest on the choruses, as well as the snare, etc. You can also use dynamics to have different instruments become the primary focus of the track from section to section. During the first verse, you might rely on the piano. During the choruses, the guitar takes over, and verse two finds the organ out front. Be sure to listen to musical models for examples and ideas.

Vocal Interference

As you construct parts, using counterpoint and dynamics, considering timbres and using the exquisite taste that only you can provide, try to be aware of what the vocal(s) will be doing. Usually, the voice is the most important instrument on your track, so parts that compete with the voice are problems. (You can test this simply by singing along with the track and listening for fights—better is to print a rough vocal that shows the phrasing and melody that's intended.) Most often, the cure is simple: Change the offending part! Sometimes, you may prefer to change the vocal line(s), but beware of weakening the vocal melody. When in doubt, *don't change the vocal melody!*

Options Open—Options Closed

One of the by-products of all the technology that's available today is the ability to keep your options open for a long time during the creative process. If you've got the tracks, you can record lots of vocal passes and wait until mix time to decide which bits to use. The same applies to guitar solos, sequenced parts—any performance may seem to justify doing another pass or two and deciding later.

This used to be the way I operated. The problem was, I got into the habit of putting off so many decisions for so long that I was overwhelmed come mix time. If this is you, take note: Close your options early rather than late. Go ahead and put off decisions you're too tired or overloaded to make, but you'll find that deciding early streamlines the process.

INSTRUMENT TRACKING

The backbone of your track will almost always be instruments, from those that are played by humans to those that are played by computer. There are special considerations to be given to each, as well as some special techniques to make track building easier. As always, these techniques aren't meant to be the last word, so feel free to adapt them however you wish.

Printing Sequenced Parts

Sometimes, it's a good idea to print the sequenced parts to tape rather than have the sequencer chasing the multitrack machine. This is the best approach when you're dealing with synth sounds that are layered—two or more synths deep. For example, let's say you're using a bass sound that uses an old mono analog synth mixed with a sample of a bass guitar. Every time you set up to work on this song, you'll have to set up this mixture, and the problem compounds if you're using layering for other sounds in your track. The solution is to print the mixed sounds to tape, making calling up the song a much easier process—assuming that you've got the tape tracks to spare.

It's also a good idea to print a "work track" of sequenced parts. I do this once my basic MIDI arrangement (drums, bass, piano) is complete, and I've got a basic mix I can work with. I usually print these tracks (in stereo if you have the tracks, mono otherwise) knowing that I'll redo them come mix time. The advantages are that when I want to work on the song, I don't have to get the computer going, select the sounds, set up a mix, etc.—it's already done. If I'm recording a vocal, I don't have to deal with the brief delay caused by the computer chasing time code each time I start the tape, and my control room is much quieter with the computer shut off. This is a great help when using a mic in the control room.

Sampler Techniques

One of the big technological breakthroughs of the last decade is digital sampling. Without going too deeply into it, the *digital sampler* is simply a recorder that allows easy manipulation of sounds. Before samplers, if you wanted to reverse a sound, you recorded it on tape and then flipped the reels so that the tape played backwards. If you wanted to change the pitch of the sound, you varied the speed of the tape machine—slower for lower pitch, faster for higher. In the early seventies, keyboard instruments that had a playback-only tape machine for each note were developed to provide realistic orchestral sounds. You pushed a note, and a piece of tape with a prerecorded sound (usually strings) was pulled over a tape head. Soon after these instruments appeared, their owners wanted different sounds, such as vocal *ooohs* and *aaahs*. The process of making specialized tapes was expensive, and the machines themselves were difficult to keep running because of their mechanical complexity. The machines were also quite expensive. Because of this, only wealthy pop stars could afford to use them to their fullest advantage.

Enter sampling. Once again, the expense ($100,000!) meant that only the seriously solvent could afford them, but since the tape mechanisms had been replaced by electronic circuitry, the reliability issue was much less of a problem. As the cost of the circuitry came down, the availability of the instruments increased, until today, samples are cheap enough for almost anyone to afford. The most common usage for samplers remains that of playing back recordings of other instruments — strings, drums, guitars, saxophones, gongs — you name it, and it's probably available for sampler owners. The basic uses of samplers only scratch the surface of the machine's capabilities, so let me suggest some uses you might not have considered.

1. Flying parts. If you have a great vocal performance on one chorus, you can record it in your sampler, and "fly" it to the other choruses. All you have to do is assign the sound to a MIDI note, and sequence that note at the appropriate place to trigger playback. You can also use this technique to thicken backing vocals. Record three parts of backups, set up a mix you like, and sample it. When you fly the mixed parts back in, you can make the part sound twice as thick by flying it in — two times on two different tracks. You'll end up with six voices (3×2). The trick here is to fly the parts in differently from each other by detuning one part slightly sharp and the other part slightly flat. You should also have the flat part start slightly sooner and the sharp part start slightly later. This will even out the timing differences that are a natural occurrence of pitch change. (When you detune sharp, you are asking the sampler to play back faster; when you detune flat, the sampler plays back slower.)

2. Move parts around. What if the vocal performance is great overall, but comes "out of the pocket" — rushing or dragging — on a few lines? Sample the offending line, assign it to a MIDI note, and shift the note around with your sequencer. Once you've got the feel where you want it, reprint the line.

3. Save your effects. If you have only a few effects, you can maximize their use by sampling the sounds that need to be effected *with the effects*. For example, decide on a snare drum sound and reverb, and record the composite sound into the sampler. Use this sample for the snare part in your song. Your reverb unit is now free to be

used on a different setting on a different instrument.

4. Build MIDI layers. If you've built a sound that uses eight synths, you can sample the composite sound and use it instead. This frees up your synths for other parts.

5. Create rhythm loops. Start by sampling a measure of an existing groove, which can then be triggered from a sequencer each measure. You'll have to adjust the tempo of the sequencer or the pitch of the sample to get the timing to match—once you're done, the sample should be able to "loop" continuously. Use this loop as a basis for a track, adding other MIDI parts, more loops, vocals, guitars, etc.; or add the loop to an already existing track.

These ideas should get you started. Also, be sure to try making your own sampled sounds rather than relying on the standard libraries that everyone uses. Make samples of yourself singing *oooh*, or of weird sounds you like. By using your own creations, you'll guarantee uniqueness in your tracks.

Subliminal Parts

Not all parts are meant to be heard—some are meant to be felt. I call these parts "subliminal," since they usually aren't noticeable until they're taken out. For example, I might use a really low organ note droning through the choruses of a song; at mixdown, I barely shade the part in, since all I want is the low-end warmth it provides. If I've done my job properly, the choruses appear fuller for no apparent reason. (This trick is also very useful if the bass instrument is forced to play in a higher register because of the key of the track—on an electric bass, the lowest note is an *E*, so playing a song in the key of *D* means that the bass will be playing in a higher register. Adding a low keyboard an octave below the played bass part will give the weight that's missing.)

Once you're hip to this concept, you'll find plenty of opportunities to put it to use. There is a danger (isn't there always?) of overusing this kind of thing, so be aware of the thin line between "creative sound sculpting" and simply being "slick."

ROUGH MIXES

Every time you finish a session on a particular song, it's a good idea to make a rough mix, usually on cassette. You'll be able to check out your work on other systems, such as your car stereo, and you'll be able to make decisions regarding what to do next at your leisure. If you own your own studio, this will save you lots of time resetting up a track just to listen to it, and if you're using a studio for hire, you'll save money. Rough mixes are invaluable before and after vocal sessions (before, to help the singer learn the song; after, to check out the performance and to plan for backup vocals).

Another good reason to do rough mixes is to practice for the real mix; trying out certain reverbs, delays and other effects. Sometimes things that seemed like a great idea at the studio sound terrible a few days later; just as often, something that seemed questionable sounds better after a few days.

I have a major warning for you about rough mixes: Don't play them for *anyone* who isn't involved with your project. The reason is simple — most people do not understand work that is "in progress." At the very best, an outsider will compliment you a little bit; more likely, you'll get a reaction that takes energy and enthusiasm away from you and allows that person to form an opinion about your work that will be difficult to change. Remember: Rough mixes are by their nature unfinished, so keep them within your circle of support.

PRODUCING INDIVIDUAL PERFORMANCES

When someone is performing, it often helps for someone else (you?) to produce. Here's the job: Give focused encouragement, enthusiasm and instruction to the performer. Encouragement and enthusiasm are extremely helpful to the performer and to the overall mood in the studio. Instruction can be a little trickier. Useful instruction is clear, precise, and relevant to the performer's capabilities.

Here's an example: "OK. Sounds really great. There's a little problem on the last note of the first phase — I'm not sure if it fits in the chord the piano is playing there. Can you try something else?" In this case, the performer can examine what he's playing on the last note of the first phase and come up with alternatives.

Now, here's an example of bad production in the same situation. "Umm, sounds OK, I think, but there's something wrong, I'm not sure where or why, it's just too . . . green or something. Can you make it more orange? You know what I mean?"

Pity the poor performer who has to figure out what this producer wants. Make your instructions clear ("I like it" / "I don't like it") and precise ("the last note of the first phrase"); and don't ask the performer to do something she can't do.

RECORDING ELECTRIC GUITAR

It is the best of times, it is the worst of times; it is the age of MIDI, for better or for worse. It is the digital era, the dawn of the sampled century and the artificial intellect; the booting of the electromechanical millennium and the faxed jam session. In times such as these, it's not surprising that some of the best tricks of bygone years have been forgotten. Return with me now to the early years of the tube age, when analog was state of the art and the ozone was whole, when gas was cheap and guitars were electric.

Use Different Sounds for Each Part

One of the great things about guitars is that they all sound different. Two guitars fresh off the same production line on the same day, built by the same people with wood from the same tree will sound different. Trick number one is to use a different guitar for each guitar part you record on your demo.

If you've only got one guitar, then you can use other techniques to get different sounds for each part. These include using different pickup combinations for each track; using different amps or amp settings for each track; using different speakers or microphones for each track; recording your guitar directly; and using different eq or effects settings.

Use a Tube Amp

As far as amps go, I strongly recommend that you go the extra mile and use a tube amp. Tube amps sound warmer and less brittle than comparable transistor amps. There is no shortage of transistor amp manufacturers claiming to have "that tube sound," but I have yet to hear one that I can wholeheartedly recommend. Yes, I know, transistor amps are more reliable, less expensive and easier to lug around than tube amps. I used to use transistor amps all the time — I finally gave up and started acquiring tube amps. I now have two modern tube amps and two mid-sixties vintage tube amps. Both of the vintage amps cost less than the modern ones, and they all sound great. They also all sound different from each other, which is why I have so many amps just for recording. If you don't already have a tube amp and want to get one, start by getting a copy of *The Tube Amp Book* from Groove Tube Electronics. There's a huge amount of information about tube amps for you to absorb before you buy. Now, if you have a transistor amp that you don't like, don't rush out to sell it. Use it! Even a transistor amp (with a speaker) will usually sound better than the "tube amp" simulator in an effects box.

Use a Small Amp

You don't need a big amp to sound big. My most powerful amp is the one I almost never use. Instead, I use one of my other amps — they're each only about 30 watts, but they distort at a lower volume than the 100-watt behemoth. Once the sound is on tape, no one can tell if the amp was big or small.

Getting Good Distortion

No way around it, distortion is a major component of electric guitar. From subtle to screaming and with infinite variations in between, this is the guitarist's Holy Grail — the search for good, juicy distortion.

Bear in mind that there are several ways to generate distortion when using an amp. The first way is simplest — just turn it up! I would argue that this way is often the best, since the distortion is produced in all of the main stages of the amp — the preamp, the power amp and the speaker. The problem is that this method is *loud*, which is why a smaller amp is preferred for recording. Method number two is to produce distortion *only* in the preamp stage of the amp, using a master volume control to keep the actual volume level down. The advantage here is that the overall level can be very low to nearly a whisper, even with gobs of distortion. The main drawback is that preamp distortion has less "touch" than method number one. Play softly or loudly — it will all sound about the same through heavy preamp distortion. Method three is to use a stomp box or effects device plugged into an amp. The results you get depend on the particular box you're using, so it's difficult to categorize them. One advantage these devices may have is the ability to create distortions no amp or preamp can.

A Really Old Trick

When you are miking an amp to be recorded, remember one of the oldest recording tricks around: Distance equals depth. This means that the closer you mike the amp, the more "up front" it will sound, and the farther back you mike it, the more room ambience you'll be recording along with the sound of the amp. This front-to-back depth can make your whole tape sound bigger. Again, use different miking distances for each guitar part.

Microphone Placement

Where you mike the amp will greatly affect the sound. Generally, the outer edge of the speaker will sound duller than the center, so try moving the mic toward the center rather than reaching for the eq when you need a brighter sound. By moving the mic around while the amp is being played, you can find "sweet spots"—areas that sound best to you. Be sure to experiment with several mics to find the best-sounding one for the particular amp you're using.

"Turn That Damn Thing Down . . ."

If you are recording in your home, you may need to control the volume of your amp in order to keep your neighbors happy. One way to do this is to use a separate speaker cabinet that is acoustically isolated from the rest of the world. If the speaker cabinet is small, such as a single 12″ speaker, you can put the cabinet inside a large cardboard box that is lined with foam rubber. Leave the front of the speaker uncovered, set up a microphone, and cover the whole thing with heavy blankets. If the speaker/box is set up in a closet, you'll get even more isolation. If your cabinet is too big for a cardboard box, you can simply put the cabinet in a closet and surround it with foam and blankets. If you have extra gear—keyboard and guitar cases, racks, or even storage boxes filled with old clothes, you can use them to provide even more isolation. By the time you're done, the cabinet will be buried in sound-deadening material, so try to leave some easy access to the microphone—after all, you're going to need to adjust it from time to time. This setup works with a separate speaker only: Don't do this to your amp—*it needs ventilation*. If you ignore this advice, be prepared to spend lots of dough repairing your amp and repairing the fire damage to your home.

Recording Guitar Direct

When you record guitar directly, you plug the guitar straight into your mixer, bypassing the amp and speaker completely. In a pinch, you can plug directly into the line input of an input channel, but since the guitar puts out less than line level, you'll get a bit of noise.

A better way is to use a direct box. You plug your guitar into the direct box, and the signal is converted from high-impedance instrument level to low-impedance line level. The output of the direct box is an XLR connector, and it is plugged into the mic input of an input channel. There are two basic types of direct boxes: passive and active (which require power from either a battery or a phantom power supply). Passive direct boxes are cheaper, but active boxes usually sound better. When buying a direct box, be sure to compare sound quality—like everything else, different direct boxes sound different. Direct guitar can sound really boring at first, so effects and eq are almost mandatory. I love the sound of direct guitar with lots of compression, eq (highs boosted and mids cut), chorusing and reverb/delay.

Direct recording of electric bass is almost the standard, and the procedure is more or less the same as recording direct guitar, though you probably won't want to use the same effects and eq. You'll get a cleaner sound if you can avoid effects altogether.

Recording Guitar With Preamps

An additional way to get a guitar signal "directly" into your mixer is to plug into a preamp first. Start by looking at the back panel of your guitar amp or preamp—does it have a "direct" or "recording" output jack? If so, you can try plugging from that output to an input channel on your board. Don't be surprised if the sound you get is vastly different from the way the amp sounds through a speaker.

The latest breed of separate guitar preamp is a combination guitar preamp and multi-fx device (they won't make any sound on their own without being plugged into a power amp and speaker). Some of these boxes even have tubes in the actual preamp stage. The advantage they offer is quite good sound quality with excellent sounding effects, some of which have been designed specifically for electric guitar. These specialized effects might include noise reduction and speaker simulation. If you are an absolute tone purist, you won't want to use one of these boxes as an amp replacement unless you're on a very tight schedule (they do make for fast and versatile recording—lots of sounds quickly), or you're sick of carrying several amps around. While the tones available may be quite good, there is still no substitute for a great-sounding amp running through a great-sounding speaker being recorded with a great mic.

Dealing With Noise

Whether you are recording with an amp or directly, noise can be a problem, especially if the part being recorded has rests all the way through it. If you have started with a clean tape track (no sound recorded yet), you can punch in and out at the appropriate times — at mixdown, the rests will be silent. If the guitar signal itself is noisy, you should spend some time trying to minimize it. If you have hum, experiment with reversing the polarity on the amp or using a ground lifting plug. If the noise is coming from the guitar, such as radio signal or other airborne interference, try to find a position in the room where you pick up the least noise. If you (or whoever is holding the guitar) turn around in a circle while listening to the noise, you should be able to find the angle that has the least noise. Remember also that anything with a microprocessor in it puts off some electromagnetic interference (nowadays, almost every piece of gear seems to have a built-in microprocessor), so move the guitar away from any computers, keyboards, effects, TV screens and wired remote controls. If you still have too much noise, you should consider getting a single-ended noise reduction unit, such as a Rocktron Hush. (*Single-ended* means that the device will work with a normal signal as opposed to an *encoded* signal, such as the noise reduction used in tape recorders.) These units will definitely get rid of most of your noise problems, although they will also change the sound quality of any signal you run through them. In many cases, this compromise is worth it.

Effects: To Print or Not to Print

Very often it's a good idea to record the effects you're using with the guitar. The advantages are that you'll free up the effects you're printing so they can be used for other sounds at mixdown time, and you won't have to go through the work of recreating the sound you already know you want. The main disadvantages are that once an effected track is on tape, it can't be uneffected without re-recording, and, if the effects you are using are stereo, you either have to use two tracks (wasteful) or print in mono (major sonic compromise). Your own recording situation will give you the answer as to whether you should print the effects or not. Do you have plenty of tracks? (Yes.) Print. Do you need the effect for another sound at mixdown? (Yep.) Print. Was the effect very difficult to create? (Uh-huh.) *Print!* Is the effect an integral part of the sound? (Si.) Print.

Bonus Tip for Guitarists Only!

Here's a final trick for you guitarists, and it's one of my favorites. Use a little baby oil for lubrication on the neck and strings of your guitar. The oil will cut down on string corrosion caused by your acid-seeping fingers, as well as making your neck slick and your hands soft as a baby's bottom. If you have an unfinished neck, the oil will be absorbed into the wood, so be warned. Also, *be sure to clean your hands of any oil before you touch the tape recorder.* If you get oil on your machine or tape, you're dead meat.

PUNCHING IN

Punching in is entering the record mode when the tape is moving (it's also common to call entering record from play on a MIDI sequencer "punching in"). The point of recording this way is to keep part of a performance you like and replace parts you don't like. If you get good at punching, you can create very solid, seamless performances—if you don't do a good job, the performances will sound . . . punched! Here's how to master this technique.

Know What Noises Your Machine Makes When Punching

Every type of tape machine punches differently. Some make an audible *click* or *pop* when they enter and/or exit record mode. Some enter record mode perfectly well, only to make a nasty noise when they exit. If you have a good idea what your machine will do, you can plan in advance to hide the noise. If your machine clicks upon entering record, try to punch *on* the beat; if the click is very sharp sounding, you may have to hide it on a snare beat.

Compensate for Punch-in Delay

All machines have a punch-in delay. You may punch at just the right moment, but the machine will be so slow that the punch is missed. Practice punching in until you have a feel for how much delay you'll be dealing with; later, when you're in a crucial session, you'll be able to compensate. It can be difficult to punch at the right point when the delay forces you to punch between the easier subdivisions of the beat, or even out of the meter of the song. In cases like this, I make a mental note of the closest beat before the punch-in one (one ee and uh, two ee and uh, three EE!), and go for it. You'll probably mess up your fair share of punches, but you'll get better. Depending on your machine, you can get to be scarifyingly good.

Seamless Punches

Some machines have a feature called *seamless punching*. This allows you to punch in the middle of a sound or syllable without any glitches. If your machine has seamless punch capability, you'll be able to do such tricks as re-recording just the *ch* on the word *touch*. Once again, the trick here is to have your timing down; also, be sure to have the singer sing along with the previously recorded track before the punch-in occurs.

Trick Your Machine

Most tape machines manuals tell you something like, "to stop recording, press the *stop* button." What they neglect to tell you is that the punch *out* delay may be long enough to erase that next phrase you intended to keep. I have found ways to trick various machines into getting out of record more quickly. On one machine, I tried hitting fast forward to stop recording—the tape lifters picked the tape up off the heads, and recording stopped more quickly than simply hitting stop. As well as that worked, hitting fast forward worked even better, I guess, because the tape lifters were aided by reversing the direction the tape was moving. On my next machine, hitting fast forward or reverse to punch out put a really nasty noise on the tape. Since the machine already punched out faster than my old machine, I wasn't too concerned, until the stop button on the new machine's remote control began to malfunction—the machine just stayed in record. Yikes! The solution I found was to use the machine's autolocate function, setting a locate point before the punch-in point, then selecting *locate 1* to get out of record. The cool thing about developing this technique is that I inadvertently stumbled on a way to get out of record quickly *and* relocate to the appropriate point to either listen or try again with only one key-stroke. Now, even though the stop button is fixed, I still use the *locate 1* button.

The best way to find out how to trick your particular machine is to try something and notice what happens. Be creative.

Tight Punches

Tight punches require focus and virtuoso timing. If you're a musician, the skills you already have developed will help you "peform" a tight punch. Tight punching requires the highest level of skill from an engineer, and it's a skill that will come only after lots of practice. I learned only by being asked to—I thought the person requesting the tight punch was crazy. Not only did I make that punch, I made others even tighter. Since then, I've hardly found a punch I couldn't make. Remember though: You're at the mercy of your machine's limitations.

Automated Punches

Some machines have automated punch-in capability—you can set the point where the machine should begin recording and where it should end. Listen to a practice run if you wish, then start and let the machine do the dirty work. I don't use this technique very much for one reason: it is very time consuming. If I had a very tight punch that I couldn't get any other way, I might use automated punch-in, but I've found that I've gotten good (and fast) enough at manual punching not to have to bother with automation. I do routinely use automated punch-*out*, since getting out of record on my machine seems to be tougher than getting in.

Using a Footswitch

Most recorders allow using a footswitch to punch in. If you are the performer and the engineer and you want to punch a certain part, a footswitch may be the only way for you to get the job done, particularly if you are playing an instrument. There are a couple of things to be aware of. First, the footswitch will punch in and out more slowly than using the machine's front or remote control panel. For this reason, I often use the footswitch to punch in and an automated loop function to punch out. I set the location, and the tape machine stops recording and rewinds to another point when my punch-out point is reached. Second, the footswitch may make a noise when you use it. (This time I don't mean electronic noise, but actual noise made by the switch that a live microphone could pick up.) If this is the case, learn how to operate the switch quietly (squeeeeze it . . .), or cover it with a towel, or even move it away from any live mics.

Cleaning a Punch

If you've tried a particular punch several times and noticed that the first recorded section of the punch sounds like two people singing, you will have to redo the punch. Before you do, you must "clean" the punch by punching in without the singer singing. Listen back to the spot again. Do you still hear a sound where you thought you had recorded silence? If so, you didn't punch in soon enough. Try it again, but be very careful not to erase anything earlier than the spot you want to clean. If you are in a really tight spot that needs to be cleaned, try using the varispeed to slow the machine down. That should give you some breathing room. Once the punch is clean, return to normal speed and resume recording.

When Your Machine Can't Punch Out Cleanly

. . . you'll have to find a *hole* (unrecorded spot) to get out. If you're recording bass guitar or some other part that simply doesn't stop once it starts, you'll just have to keep recording until the end. Sorry.

Some Artistic Considerations

When punching a vocal, guitar or other live-instrument track, be careful about continuity. By this I mean make sure that the sound, the intensity, and the performance of the voice or instrument doesn't change drastically at the punch. With vocalists, it's a good idea to give enough running room for the singer to get the mood and the groove and the timbre right before the punch in. Be careful not to give too much time before the punch—you may lose the singer's interest. Ask the singer to sing along as soon as he knows where he is so that his voice is up and running—this will also help any noise gates or compressors do what they would have been doing on a single take. Some singers will change their approach during a punch; for example: The line you want to punch ends with a sustained vowel sound, then there's an instant for a breath, then the next line begins. If the singer knows that you'll be punching out after the sustained note and that he won't need to breathe to get the next line, he may "milk" that last note. The result is either an unbelievable performance (no singer on earth could really sing all of this on one breath) or worse—accidental erasure of part of the next line. Ask the singer to sing as if he were continuing after the punch-out, breaths and all. Another bad habit you may run into is the singer who emphasizes either the punch-in or -out point. Once again, just ask the singer to sing the lines before, during and after the punch points as if they were all part of the same performance.

When you listen back, check the performance carefully. Does the performance flow from line to line, or does the attitude change suddenly at the punch? Does the timbre or the level change? If the performance is stellar, but the timbre changes, see if you can compensate with a little eq — you may be able to turn on that setting for just the one line. Level changes can be a drag at mixdown, but if the performance is great, keep it.

Step Three

VOCALS

LEAD VOCALS

Working With a Singer

The most important sound on your finished tape is the lead vocal — that's what the listener hears first, so you've got to have a great vocal if your tape is to be a success. You'll need all your communication skills as well as your musical skills to do a good job — after all, drum machines and computers can't reason and rarely get offended by what you ask of them. Singers and other performers are different. For one thing, you will often have only one opportunity to record that magical performance, and you'll have to make decisions very quickly. You will also need to be very specific about any adjustments you'd like the singer to make, and you'll have to do all this in a fashion that encourages teamwork. Your concentration level, as well as your diplomacy, must be at its highest. (Should you fail in your mission, I will disavow all knowledge of you. This tape will self-destruct in fifteen seconds. . . .)

As usual, preparation is important, so:

Make Several Typed Lyric Sheets

Typed lyric sheets are essential for a vocal session; they'll help both you and the singer know where you are, and help you keep track of which takes are good. Double spacing helps, but it's not necessary. You'll need one copy for the singer (she will also need a pencil to make notes, and a music stand to set the lyrics on); one copy for each person helping with the session (engineer, songwriter, etc.); and one copy for each track the lead vocal will be recorded on. As you record and play back, you can use your pencil to put check marks next to each line that sounds really good.

Record the First Take
You already know this, don't you? Even if you're still setting levels, put the machine into record. What have you got to lose? Only a potentially great performance! Don't tell the singer you've started recording, just do it.

Provide Beverages
This may seem obvious, but if you aren't prepared, you'll waste time and disrupt the flow by going for water right in the middle of the session. Singers need water—lots of it. Some want warm water, some want coffee or tea or hot water, and none that I have worked with drink alcoholic beverages at sessions.

Have Your Guide Vocal Handy
You may need to refer to the guide vocal in order to explain something to the singer. If you've got the spare tracks, you can just listen to the guide track that's on the multitrack master. If you needed to erase the guide track in order to record the lead vocal, you'd better have the rough cassette mix ready to go. By the way, if you are recording over the guide vocal track:

Clean Any Tracks Before You Record Over Them
It's a good idea to clean (record over with no input—just unplug the appropriate input cable at the tape machine and record) guide tracks before recording something new over them. (Be sure you want to get rid of the guide track; it's gone forever once it passes over the erase head.) Not only will you be sure that the erasure is complete, you'll also find that it's easier to deal with a track that contains only what you want. Besides, erasing small portions of a track is a nerve-wracking pain; can you imagine accidentally erasing some of the lead vocal along with remnants of the old guide track?

The Headphone Mix
Since my studio is a one-room affair, I almost always have to record with the singer in the same room as me. This makes headphones a must for both me and the singer. I set up the headphone mix that we'll use, and then ask for suggestions from the singer—does he need more track, more reverb, whatever? I try to keep the headphone volume low for a number of reasons: First, loud phones will leak sound into the microphone and be recorded along with the

vocal; second, ear fatigue caused by too-loud phones makes it harder to judge what's being recorded; third, I have blown up phones before; fourth, and most importantly, I prefer not to permanently damage anyone's ears.

I also use as few effects as possible when recording a vocal. Of course, I *never* print effects on a vocal track, but beyond that consideration, I find that using reverb, delay, chorusing, etc. muddies things to the point that I can't hear pitch problems when they occur. I seldom even use any effects on the track while I'm recording vocals—I want as few sonic distractions as possible between me and the voice. Many singers need the reassurance of hearing reverb when they sing. If so, give it to them. Others know that using little or no reverb will allow them to really focus on their pitch and timbre.

Dealing With Pitch Problems

It's a fact of life: Some singers have problems singing in key. Sometimes the problem is slight, sometimes not. There are a few things you can try to help in this situation. First, try turning off the reverb, as I pointed out above. Next, try changing the level of the vocal in relation to the track. You see, if the vocal is too loud, the singer will not hear enough of the track to use as a pitch reference. When that happens, the tendency is to listen too closely to the voice, and to use it as the pitch reference, usually resulting in the singer's singing sharp. If the vocal is too quiet in relation to the track, the singer can't tell what she's doing, which often causes the singer to sing flat. I have worked on several different occasions with singers who were able to adjust their pitch by changing the level of the voice heard in the phones. If that doesn't work, try having the singer remove one side of the headphones away from her ear, so that she hears herself in the room as well as in the phones.

In some extreme cases, the singer will be paying so much attention to his voice that he can't seem to ever sing in tune. He will listen to every nuance, analyzing his performance as it happens, and messing himself up in the process. In cases like this, I have gone so far as to remove the vocal from the headphone mix, forcing the singer to forget about himself and to focus on the track. Like magic, his pitch often improves. I can then play back what we've just recorded, and show him that when he listens less to himself, his performance improves. This situation is rare and will require extreme sensitivity when you discuss it with the singer. Remember, singers need lots of encouragement, even if they have some habits you need to work around.

Sometimes, despite all your efforts, the singer cannot sing in tune. Maybe the singer is tired and simply needs some rest. It's no big deal; just have the singer come back another time.

Vocal Recording Strategies

Here's the way I like to record vocals: Have the singer sing the whole song, top to bottom, and record it. Move to a new track and do the same thing again. Repeat for as many tracks as you can spare until you feel you have the performance you want, even if that performance is spread out over several tracks. Normally, three or four tracks should suffice, but don't be afraid to use more if you've got them. If your singer is really on it and knows the song exceptionally well, you may only need one track. (Remember to leave an empty track to bounce to if you're planning to comp the vocal.) As you record each track, pay very close attention to everything—performance, pitch, extraneous noises, "*p*'s" popping, momentary distortion (the singer sang so loudly at one point that the microphone preamp overloaded), correct lyrics and melody being sung, etc. With a pencil, you can mark your lyric sheets to show sections that are good and sections that need to be replaced.

I find that performances recorded one after the other get better and better, until the singer "peaks," at which point subsequent performances get worse. I use this peak take as the basis for the final vocal. If the track needs "fixes," you'll probably find them on one of the other tracks. If not, you'll have to punch the sections that need replacement.

Some very experienced singers prefer to sing a line at a time. This is a special skill—it's very difficult to build a convincing performance this way, for both the singer and the engineer. It can be quite difficult and nerve-wracking for the engineer to do endless tight punches, since one slip will erase a section that was a keeper. The singer has to somehow make the performance sound real, as if it had occurred in one take. It's worthwhile for you to try both methods, in order to find out what works best for the particular singer you're working with.

Comping the Vocal

Comping is simply combining—taking the best sections from two or more tracks and combining them into one performance. (One singer I know says this about comping: "It's like shopping. You get something from here, and then something from there . . . .") There are two basic ways to comp. The first is to simply mute the channels with parts you don't want, and to unmute the track with the part you do. For example, if we have vocals recorded on tracks one, two and three, we might start with track three for verse one and chorus one, switch to track two for verse two and chorus two, track one for the bridge, and back to track two for the rest of the song. (It helps to mark a lyric sheet to remind you when to make the switches.) The advantage of this method is that the vocal tracks never lose a generation by being bounced. The drag is that you've got to manually do the switches, and this can be a lot of work at mixdown. If you have MIDI muting on your mixer, you can use your sequencer to automate the changes from track to track. You can get the switches to occur between words (I've been able to get tracks to switch within a single syllable without anyone being able to tell), and the sequencer will "remember" as many moves as you care to program.

If you don't have MIDI muting and you've got a lot of track switching to accomplish, use the second method, which is to record all the good sections onto a blank track. Start with verse one: Take the output of tape track you want to record and patch it directly into the comp track's input. Record the sections in verse one that you want from this track; in fact, you can simply record all of verse one over to the comp track. Now, let's say that the second line of the first verse needs to come from a different track. Plug that track's output into the comp track's input, and record just that line. If the punch is tight, you may want to rehearse it several times. If it's really tight, you can try slowing the tape machine's speed, or if your machine has it, use the auto punch feature.

By doing this all the way through the song, you will build a comp track that is the combination of all the best moments from your vocal takes. Once you're happy with the comp, you can then erase the original vocal tracks, giving you more room to record. In the process of comping, you may run into extreme level differences: One line will be at a good volume, the next will be too quiet, and the following one too loud. You can compensate for this at mix time with fader moves, or you can re-record the offending sections of the comp track. This time, you'll need to run the tape track you want to record through a mixer channel, which will allow you to adjust the level going to the comp track. Simply adjust the level to taste, and re-record each line, one at a time.

Tape Speed Techniques

If the high part is too high for the singer, try using your multitrack's pitch control to slow the tape. This will lower the pitch, making that really high note easier to reach. If you try this, be aware that the farther away from standard speed you go, the stranger the voice will sound once the tape speed is returned to normal.

Another use of the pitch control is to record some of the backups (perhaps just the doubles) at a different speed—not to make the parts easier to sing, but to subtly change the timbre of the voices you're recording. Once again, the farther from normal speed, the more extreme the effect. This also works on lead vocals—remember "Lucy in the Sky With Diamonds"?

Recording a Double

Once you have the vocal take you want (either you got a great take or you did some comping), you may want to *double track* the vocal (record another track to be used as a "thickener" at mix time) in certain sections of the song, possibly for the entire track. The quickest way to record a double is to let the singer listen to one line at a time and then record that line only. Once you get into the groove of *listen—rewind—record—(next line) listen—rewind—record* and so on, you should be able to move right along. Some singers want to hear the original vocal louder than the double; others want the double louder—give the singer whatever he needs to get the job done. You won't need to be too concerned about perfect pitch matching between the lead vocal and the double, since you'll probably set the double quieter than the lead at mix time. The phrasing of the two tracks, however, is critical. Consonants can be a big problem when they don't match perfectly, so listen carefully and be able to give very specific instructions if there are problems. In many cases, it's a good idea for the singer to soft pedal the consonants on the double track, even going so far as to leave off any *s*'s that occur at the end of a phrase. Speaking of the ends of phrases, make sure that the lead vocal and the double agree with each other regarding when a line ends—it's very audible when the double "drops out" or "hangs over" in relation to the lead.

Hiring a Demo Singer

For those of us who are songwriters trying to get our songs cut by artists other than ourselves, there comes a time when we need to hire a demo singer. Even if you are an accomplished singer yourself, you'll find that your voice isn't appropriate for every song. There are exceptions, of course. Tom Kelly sings most of his and Billy Steinberg's demos, but then again, those two already have Clive's weekend retreat phone number.

A great singer will sell a song for you. Many times I have heard songs that didn't do much for me be brought to life by the convincing performance of a demo singer. We're talking about the difference between a cut and a pass!

Here in Los Angeles, there is a sizable community of well-known demo singers. Some of these folks have record deals of their own, and they support themselves doing demos until their record comes out. We songwriters can capitalize on this situation and end up with major-league talent singing our demos.

First, you'll have to find a singer. There are lots of ways to do this — listening to other songwriter demos and asking who the vocalist is, is one of the easiest. You can also check out singers at local clubs, but unless they are already working as studio singers, you may be asking for trouble. Singing live and singing in the studio are two very different skills, and one doesn't guarantee the other.

Choose a Category

I tend to categorize demo singers — much as our demos get categorized. The categories I use are: male/female (seems obvious, doesn't it?); rock/r&b/country/alternative/folk/etc.; clear-voiced/rough-voiced; soprano/alto/tenor/baritone and so on. (I haven't yet needed a bass singer . . . .)

These categories make it easier for me to describe the voice I'm looking for when I talk to other songwriters and helps me keep a clear idea of what I'm after. If I'm pitching to Wynonna Judd, then I'll need a female country alto with a fairly clear voice; Tanya Tucker would be the same but with a rough voice. If I'm trying to get Rod Stewart to "hear" my song, I'll use a male, rough-voiced, rock tenor. By the way, if you use a singer who sounds too much like Rod Stewart, you'll have another problem — a song that's worthless to anyone else because they can't imagine anyone but Rod singing it. What if Rod says no?

Check the Range of Your Song

There are several important steps to take at the selection stage of hiring a singer. One of the most important is to check the range of the singer with the range of the song. I'm not talking about soprano/alto/tenor here. I'm saying that you need to know the specific high and low notes of the song and check with the vocalist to make sure that they are comfortably within his range. You can do this over the phone — just be sure you do it. It's also a good idea to go over each section of the song with the singer to make sure that the melody doesn't stay on the singer's *break* — the point in a singer's range where he or she switches from a chest tone to a head tone. If you run into this situation, try changing the key of the song up or down. A half step can work wonders.

Consider the Style

Once again, I'm not talking about rock/country, etc. By this I mean the specific way a singer sings within his or her genre. Sometimes it's tempting to use a vocalist whose tone is to die for, but whose style is a little out of whack for the song. We (the songwriters) tell ourselves, "It's OK, we'll show them the licks and inflections we want. . . ." This is a recipe for disaster. Altering one's singing style is very difficult and unpredictable. You may get the licks you want, and maybe even the inflections, but the performance will have no soul. The result is a demo that doesn't help the song. Neither the singer nor the writer(s) will be happy about the whole thing.

During the Session . . .

The first few minutes of a session involving a hired demo singer are the moments when the singer, the songwriter and the engineer get to know each other. Each person talks about where they're from, who they've worked with in town, do they like cats or dogs — those sorts of things. If you're the person footing the bill, you may feel funny paying people money to socialize, but the socializing serves a valuable function as long as it doesn't eat up too much time. Ten minutes usually suffices. By then, some friendly interaction has already started, and you can all get about the business of recording together.

Next, the engineer (you?) will begin running the track so that the singer can get familiar with the song. If you are the songwriter, be patient during this phase! You will hear lots of mistakes as the singer works her way through the song. Stay cool, and let the singer learn. When you hear the singer starting to settle down into the song, start working together to fine-tune the first verse and chorus, and start recording, even if you think the singer isn't quite ready. You might get lucky!

Remember Who Is Singing

If you have hired a singer, try to avoid forcing the singer to sing like you. I've seen this happen, with songwriters who can't quite pull off the vocal themselves trying to make the hired singer sing like the songwriter would sing, if only he could. I'm not saying never do this — just be flexible if the singer balks at your requests.

When Giving Instructions

Try to avoid being indecisive. I know this is a tough one, but making others wait while you make up your mind can really gum up the works. Also, you must be specific when you make suggestions to a singer. "Your last note was a little sharp," is much easier to do something about than, "It doesn't sound right."

Money

At some point, you'll be discussing money — good singers don't generally work for free. Most singers have a set rate for a demo session, regardless of hours. Some include background vocals, and others charge extra. At first, you may feel funny paying a good chunk of money for someone who breezes in and sings your tune in ninety minutes flat; after all, it's taken you xxxty hours or so to write the thing, much less record the tracks. Don't worry, soon enough you'll realize that a singer who comes in and nails a great vocal in that short a time is actually saving you money in studio time and grief in production anguish.

Producing Yourself

If you're the singer, you may end up having to produce yourself while you engineer and sing. This is a tough job, since it requires three different skills — performing, recording and analyzing the results. If you can get someone you trust to produce your vocal, you'll likely find that you get a better performance than you would have gotten on your own, since you'll be able to concentrate more fully on singing. If you produce yourself, here are some suggestions:

First, try to separate the three jobs as much as possible. Start by setting up the mic levels and headphone mix you want. Then, set up the tape and mixer tracks you'll be recording to so that you can quickly switch to a new track once you've begun to sing. Now, the only engineering chores will be to actually punch in and out, rewind, etc. Before you start singing, be sure you have lyric sheets ready, as well as any beverages you want. Turn off the phone, lock the door, and otherwise get rid of any distractions.

When you start singing, start easily in order to warm up. (If you have a warm-up procedure, use it.) Your voice will sound much better if you use a warm-up tape (such as Seth Riggs's "Singing for the Stars") before you start singing. Start recording. I suggest singing the entire song, rather than line by line, since the engineering chores during a line-by-line recording are more demanding. If you've totally blown the first take, re-record it; otherwise, move to the next track. Try your best not to analyze what you're doing—instead, focus on your performance. Once you've filled up the tracks you intended to use, stop and make rough mixes of each take to listen to later. (It helps to "label" the takes by using the talkback mic on your board, announcing "take xx" before each mix.) If you hear a line that really needs to be replaced, go ahead and punch it in if you're up to it—if not, wait until you've gone through the entire group of rough mixes. You may have the line in question on another track anyway.

When you listen to the rough mixes (try to wait at least a day before you listen: Give yourself a chance to have some perspective), make notes on separate lyric sheets (one for each take) reflecting which lines are good and which aren't. You may find that there are several lines that didn't happen on any of the takes; in this case, you'll need to re-record those lines. Spend a little time trying to get the vocal sound to be the same as it was on the first session. There will likely be some timbre differences, due to changes in your voice, among other things, but with a bit of effort you should be able to get a reasonably close match. When you punch in, be careful not to erase lines you meant to keep! Once you've got all the lines you need, comp the vocal as you normally would.

BACKING VOCALS
Backing vocals are often the final touch that makes all the difference, taking a good track and making it really sparkle. This applies no

matter what kind of music you're doing: The sound of the human voice is a powerful texture, and since every human voice is unique, you have an unlimited range of timbres to work with.

Maybe you've had some previous choral experience, in a church choir or glee club. If so, you can put some of what you've learned to use in arranging backing vocals. Even if you haven't had any formal experience, you can learn by listening to — you guessed it — musical models. In pop music, there are hundreds of styles of backing vocals, so start by listening to a style you like, since that style will be more likely to be useful to you. Have no shame — copy examples you really like; after you've done enough out-and-out copying, you'll start to combine styles and hopefully be headed toward developing your own style. (It's also fun to trace the style you're interested in backwards; for example, if you like Take Six, the a cappella vocal group, you might also want to listen to the Nylons, as well as some gospel choirs. What the heck, go listen to a church choir this Sunday — it's one of the easiest ways to hear a vocal group.)

Working Out Parts

When you're working on backing vocals for a specific song, start by working out parts. (If you have some background in harmony, it will be much easier for you to work out parts. If you don't have any experience, find a friend who can help, then watch very carefully. After a few sessions, you'll pick it up.) The way I do this is to listen to the track (or a rough mix) and play around with vocal ideas, singing along and making note of the ones that work. The possibilities are endless: How many voices? singing what syllables? parallel to the lead vocal (the same phrasing)? counterpoint (different phrasing from the lead vocal)? aaah's? oooh's? It helps to break the job down to first deciding *where* backups are needed. Next, decide on the *syllables* and *phrasing* to be used. Finally, decide on the actual *notes* to be sung. Change the order of this process if you like, and don't be concerned if your ideas don't always work — just try another one. Blind alleys are part of the deal.

Recording the Parts

Once you have your ideas together, start recording. There are several main approaches. One is to have the backing parts maintain enough character that they are almost as central to the song as the lead vocal. The Beatles as well as Simon and Garfunkel used this approach quite often; the backup vocal was nearly a duet—you could tell who the backup singer was. This is the simplest (from a recording standpoint) approach to achieve, since the backup vocal is recorded more or less the same as the lead vocal. Sometimes both the lead and the backup are doubled, but often this isn't necessary. The results are usually the most unique, since the character of the backup vocal is retained.

Another approach is to build up a large-group sound with several different voices. You can still maintain uniqueness (à la the Beach Boys or Boyz 2 Men) if you're careful about combining timbres. Even if a singer can sing the high part, she might sound better singing the middle or the low. If you're working with a group of singers, spend a little time having them switch parts, and listen for the combination that works best. If you're recording a group of voices this way, try recording all the parts at once through one microphone. You'll have to adjust the blend of the singers by having one or another move into or away from the mic—once the balance is cool, press the red button. To thicken the track, have the singers record a double on another track.

Really Big Backups

Part of the reason that backup parts on records sound so good (besides using great singers) is the doubling and tripling and even quadrupling of parts. This means the singer sings a part once, then twice, then even more times. If there are three parts and each part is tripled, you're hearing nine singers. Now, suppose you have two singers singing at the same time, and they sing each part three times; that's eighteen singers. Notice that in this arrangement style, the two singers are singing the same part simultaneously, rather than singing two different parts at the same time. Unless I'm in severe track trouble or the singers sing outstandingly well together, I almost never record two different parts on the same track, since rebalancing levels later is impossible.

Obviously, to get nine tracks of vocals on your multitrack tape, you need nine tracks. You people with only eight tracks are out of luck. Even those with sixteen tracks can be in trouble when it's time to record backups.

For this reason, it's a good idea to plan how many tracks you'll need to get the sound you want. If you need three parts, try to leave room for six tracks; that's three parts, doubled. If you have an 8-

track machine, you may need to lay down a mono work mix of your sequenced track to sing to—including your time code track, you'll have six tracks left. If you are using real instruments like guitar, record a rough guitar part that can be erased later as a vocal guide. If you've already used too many tracks, just use three vocal tracks— we'll double them later with techno-trickery. (Those of you with more tracks, great! We'll use as many as you can spare.) By the way, however many tracks you have available now, you will ultimately be using only two or four come mix time.

(If you really don't have the tracks you need, you can make a "pseudoslave" reel. Make a mix of your track onto DAT, then record this mix back onto your multitrack on a clean piece of tape. You'll now have plenty of tracks to record vocals, which you'll later fly back to the master multitrack tape.)

Record the first vocal part. Once you are happy with the results, and if you have the tracks, record the same part again on a new track. Be sure the new track "locks" with the first track—listen carefully to the consonants, particularly the *s*'s and *c*'s and *k*'s. If the parts don't match, re-record the weaker performance. Repeat this procedure with the next two parts, making sure the consonants match the previous parts as well as the same part. If you need to compromise here, try not doubling the lowest (in pitch) part, saving one track. If all of the previous steps have been successful, you should have some really good-sounding backups.

Carefully blend the vocals in stereo until they sound best to you. I usually pan the highest parts left and right, the middle parts at 9 o'clock and 3 o'clock, and the lowest parts slightly left and right of center. Be careful if one of the parts is similar or the same as the lead vocal—you'll need to have that part a bit further back in the blend. Once you're happy, record *just the vocals* onto a DAT machine (or analog 2-track ¼" mixdown machine).

Next, you'll need to fly the parts on DAT onto the multitrack tape. (You can also use a sampler to fly the parts around—see the section on "Sampler Techniques" on page 111.) If the section you've been working on is the first chorus and all the other choruses are the same, start your flying in the second chorus. This way, you can correct any blending problems you encounter. Flying vocals from DAT is easier than you may think, since the use of start id's gives you a consistent place to start playback each time. With your DAT in "pause/play," press "play" and count how many beats it takes for the sampled vocals to play. Next, reset the DAT machine, play the second chorus, and try to find the right beat to start DAT playback. You'll probably have to start playback at a subbeat to get the proper synchronization of the chorus and the vocals. Once you've found the proper beat, record the stereo vocals from the DAT onto two open tracks on your multitrack. If the vocals are late, just start DAT playback a bit sooner; if the vocals are early, start the DAT later. With a bit of luck, you'll be able to fly the vocals in perfectly. If you can spare two more tracks, fly the same vocals in yet again for an even thicker sound. If the vocals sound like they are flanging, you may want to try recording the second pass again until it sounds better. (Unless you like the flanging!) Repeat this procedure on all the other choruses, saving the first for last. At this point, you should erase the "old" original vocal tracks before you lay the DAT vocals down. If you used an analog 2-track machine, the above procedure is only slightly different. Instead of a start id (à la DAT), you'll have to mark the start on the tape with a china marker (white is easiest to see). Simply make a mark on the *back* of the tape — the back is the side that doesn't touch the surface of the heads — that is about a second before the start of the vocal section you'll be flying. This mark should be lined up at a repeatable point, say 12 o'clock on the supply reel. You can now try to find an appropriate beat to begin playback. Once you've gotten close, you'll find that your old analog machine has an advantage over DAT: Instead of you having to press "play" on an off-beat in order to be in sync, you can move the start position of the marked tape. If the 2-track is early, move the mark clockwise, from 12 o'clock to 3 o'clock. If the 2-track is late, move the start position counterclockwise, from 12 o'clock to 9 o'clock. You'll have to fine-tune the position further, but it is much easier to start playback on the beat than to start on an off-beat.

If you're on eight tracks, the only change you may need to make is to blend the original vocals in mono before recording them to DAT, and to record the DAT vocals back onto the multitrack one track at a time. The only thing you'll lose is some stereo imaging; this may not matter if you pan the two mono tracks left and right at mix time. If you opted for two pairs of stereo vocals (you sixteen-trackers), try panning the two pairs differently.

A word of warning: The *really big backups* approach is nothing if not slick, and slick isn't always the best way to go. If a simple approach sounds great and takes less time, use it!

Step Four

MIXING

An engineer friend of mine once told me, "Mixing is God's gift to engineers." This is the time when all your work comes together, when the bits of sound you began constructing are combined into a whole piece. Here's how I go about getting a great mix.

FINAL TRACKING AND MIX PREP

Try your best to be finished tracking *before* your start mixing; otherwise, you'll be getting ear fatigue too early into the process, and your mix will suffer. If you've got just a bit of tracking left to do, such as a vocal line to replace, do it in a separate session — one I call the "mix prep." Since there's often a bit of organizing to do before the actual mix begins, I find that I'm best combining all of these chores so that when the mix begins there's nothing left to do *but* mix. So, finish up any tracking you have to do. Next, do any premixing you have to do. What's *premixing*? This is when you combine several tracks (such as backing vocals) down to a single track or a stereo pair. (If you've been using a stereo work track, you can put the premixed vocals there, since you won't be needing the work track anymore. Be sure to clean the work track before you record it.) The reason to do a premix is to avoid lots of minute level corrections during the mix, as well as to maximize the sheer amount of sounds you can fit on your multitrack. Often, you will have been doing premixes all the way through the process of making your demo, so anything you're doing now is really a final step.

If you have any comping to do, such as lead vocal or solo tracks, do it now. (See "Comping the Vocal" in Step Three — Vocals.)

You'll also need to clean up your master, erasing any performances you're sure you won't need later. The exception here is lead vocal tracks — keep all of them if you can. The best way to clean tracks is simply to record with nothing plugged into the input of the track you're erasing. *Be very careful* not to get rid of a performance you want to keep.

If you have home-studio-style automation (such as MIDI muting and MIDI control of effects), the mix prep session is a good time to get it all happening. Let's face it—automation is nerd work (yes, I'm a nerd, and you're one too, if you spend as much time in front of a computer as I do). Get the nerd work over with so you can focus on making sonic decisions once the mix begins.

Set the Master Fader

The ideal position for the master fader is 0 dB. The problem is that by the time you've dialed in your mix, your meters will be showing a good bit more than 0 dB. The reason for this is that we all tend to adjust individual levels upwards to compensate for what we hear. "Okay, let's add some more acoustic guitar. Great. Oh, now we need a little more kick and snare. Now, just add a pinch more bass. . . ." You get the idea. Before you've finished, your meters will be cooking, and your board is not sounding its best. Knowing this situation will occur leads to how to beat it—start with your master fader higher than you think you need it. That way, when levels get out of control, you can pull the master back down to 0 dB, and still have some adjustment room. If you don't take this precaution, you may find that the only way to get levels under control again is to pull every fader down about the same amount, and that means the mix will have changed. When you start out with this trick, you'll probably overdo it, but with time, you'll learn what initial setting works for you. (I personally start with the master fader about 5 dB hot.)

Label the Board

If you're working with eight or more tracks, you should label the channels on your board. You could use a china marker and write directly onto your mixer, but removing the china marker's marks is difficult. The best solution is removable tape—¾" or so wide. (There's a version of masking tape called *drafting tape* that works fine, or you can use the more expensive, white removable stuff.) You can write directly on the tape and remove it when the mix is done. You can even save the labeled tape in case of a remix later on.

MIXING TECHNIQUE

Start Mixing With No Effects or EQ

Every once in a while, I get asked to help mix someone else's tape at his home studio. When I ask to hear what he's got so far, I usually find that every channel is set with an extreme amount of eq and reverb. The first thing I do is turn it all off so I can hear what I'm really dealing with. It's easy to make a mess of a mix by reaching for the eq and the reverb too soon. Start out with all eq set flat and all effects off. Add either only when you need to.

Build Your Mix From the Drums Up

I almost always start with the drums — they provide the foundation, and they usually stay fairly steady throughout the whole song. Bring up just the kick and listen. You may be tempted to add eq and reverb, but wait just a bit. Next, add the snare. Once you are happy with the relationship of the kick and snare, add the high hat. At this point, you're still just setting levels, pulling down any sounds that are too loud and boosting those that need help. (If you have difficulty setting these levels, try comparing them with an appropriate track from a CD.)

Next, I usually set up a basic reverb for the snare. My standard starting point is a medium-sized room with a 50- to 100-ms predelay. I also usually take some of the low end out of the reverb, with the eq built into the reverb unit. I then adjust the decay setting of the reverb based on the tempo of the song, leaving a long-enough reverb "tail" on the snare without the reverb playing over the next snare hit. (If you let the reverb last too long, your mix will be muddier.) Once I'm happy with the snare reverb, I might add a shade of reverb into the kick. I generally don't use the same reverb as the snare, since the kick will most often be playing notes that the snare isn't, and the reverb "tails" will overlap. Since I don't want to dedicate one reverb to the kick alone, I'll usually send the kick through my main vocal reverb, using the least amount I can get away with. Once I'm happy with what I've got, I add the bass instrument, since it also usually plays through the whole song.

Notice that there are still drums to add in — toms, cymbals, percussion, etc. The only time I add any of these instruments in before the bass is when they play more-or-less constantly through the whole song, such as a tom or conga rhythm. Otherwise, I try to get the bass, kick, snare and hat to "agree" with each other before adding the rest of the rhythm section. Once you've achieved this agreement, go ahead and add the rest of the percussive instruments.

Some of these remaining rhythm-section instruments will also require some reverb. Congas and other percussion can go into the main vocal reverb, as can the cymbals; however, I find most often that very little if any reverb is really necessary. Toms can go into the snare reverb unless they interfere with the snare too much or if they require a specific effect. If so, you'll need another reverb/fx device to handle them. As I say, you can't have too many reverbs.

If you don't have enough reverbs and you need to do something dramatic with the toms (or other percussion instruments), you can set up the effect and print to tape. This assumes that you have tracks to spare. If you don't have the tracks, there's still another way to get what you want if your snare reverb is MIDI controllable. At the most basic level, you can set up two MIDI patches, one for the snare reverb, and one for the toms. You can then switch between the two with a MIDI program change from your sequencer, or for those who don't use MIDI, with a footswitch. You may have to compromise a bit if there is a section where both the snare and toms play — in this instance, try leaving one patch or the other active through the passage in question, or remove the offending snare beats. If none of this works, go borrow another reverb from a friend!

You can now continue adding instruments, starting with the ones that play through most of the song; perhaps it's the piano and acoustic guitars, or maybe it's the brass section. In any case, continue adding instruments, with the exception of solo or lead instruments. Don't add vocals yet.

Now, listen to the song from the top. This is the time to start adding eq and effects, but be sure to work on only one sound at a time — otherwise, you'll get confused. Once you've achieved the blend you want, you can move on to working on the vocals and solo instruments.

Position Your Pan Pots

Unless you're mixing in mono, you'll need to decide where to position your sounds with the pan pots. Generally, the most important sounds on your track will be centered — kick, snare, lead vocal, etc. It's all too easy to put too much in the center; then you may as well be mixing to mono! Using your pan pots creatively will open up your mixes, and even affect balance decisions you'll be making. It helps to listen to other recordings to hear the effect of panning and placement.

The bass instrument is usually centered for a few reasons. The main one is that bass frequencies are much less directional than mid and high frequencies; if you play a very low note (with no overtones) through a speaker that is hidden from view, it will be quite difficult to hear exactly where the note is coming from. A mid- or high-frequency sound is much more easily located by the listener. An additional factor is that low frequencies require bigger speakers and more power to reproduce—since something panned to the center is coming through two amplifiers and speakers, it will be much more able to be reproduced cleanly. There is also the factor of habit— bass sounds have nearly always been centered since the introduction of stereo, when vinyl LP's were the medium of choice. LP's were simply unable to provide much separation at low frequencies. (By the way, none of this should stop you from positioning the bass anywhere you want.)

Instruments that have been doubled can be panned opposite each other; not just hard left and right, but in between settings as well. Using a clock face for a reference, try panning doubled sounds at 10 and 2 o'clock, or 9 and 3. Got it? Bear in mind that the farther left or right an instrument is placed, the easier it is to hear. This means that as you move a sound away from the center, you may be able to turn it down slightly in the mix and still be able to hear it just fine.

Skillful use of the pan pots will help you to "unclutter" a busy mix or add drama to a lifeless one. If you get brave, you can even move the position of an instrument as it is playing—just like Jimi Hendrix did in 1968. (Sounds great through headphones. . . .)

Make Repeatable Moves

Throughout the mix, you'll be adjusting various things; turning instruments up or down, changing a pan location, swelling a reverb or changing effects levels. Each of these adjustments is called a *move*. The easiest moves to make are those that require turning something on or off, such as turning on a channel of your mixer just before the solo comes in. This concept can be expanded in some cool ways, depending on the move you'd like to accomplish and the switches on your particular mixer. Need to make the snare reverb lots louder at a certain point? Try switching the snare channel's reverb send from "postfader" to "prefader." As long as the fader is less than wide open, this simple switching will drastically increase the amount of snare signal sent to the reverb. Maybe your board has six effects sends controlled by five knobs; one knob sends to one of two effects (let's say sends three and four), selected by a switch. If you leave one of these two sends disconnected (number three), the switch becomes an on/off switch for the remaining send (number four). When you want an instrument sent to the effect, you simply select the appropriate send. When you want to remove an instrument from an effect, you just select the disconnected send (number three).

Sometimes you need to adjust several faders at once. If it's just a pair of faders, you can use two fingers to make the adjustment. More faders mean more fingers. This technique works, so long as the faders are all in relatively the same position. If you need to adjust four faders upward by 10 dB at the same time, but each fader has a different initial setting, your fingers may not be able to do the job. In this case, use the palm of your hand laid flat across all four faders—it takes some practice, but you'll be able to make the move without breaking any fingers.

Activate Switches On the Beat

When turning a switch on or off you may find that noise is created. This can happen when the switch is dirty, or when a very loud signal is going through the switch. Sometimes the noise is caused when you are switching a reverb from one size room to another; this kind of noise is unavoidable, but it can be hidden. To hide any noise that may occur when throwing a switch, simply make your move on the beat—snare drums and cymbal crashes work great.

Mixing the Lead Vocal

As you know, the lead vocal is usually the most important element of your mix—if you don't get it right, your mix won't fully succeed. It also takes experience to get the lead vocal sounding its best and sitting properly in the track. A good place to start, once again, is to listen to an appropriate recording: If you're working on a country ballad with a clear-sounding female soprano, you'll need to find a recording you like with a similar singer. It also helps if the other instruments in the track are similar to the track you're mixing. In any case, listen to how the vocal sounds—listen to the reverb and any other effects. You don't need to exactly copy the sound you hear, but comparing your mix to the one on the CD will make it much easier for you to achieve a good mix.

How a vocal sounds affects how loud it appears in a mix—if the vocal is a little dull sounding, it may get lost. If it's too bright, the voice may jump out of the mix. If there are too many dynamic differences (loud parts too loud, soft parts too soft), mixing the voice in properly will be very difficult. Let's deal with these situations.

Lead-Vocal Compression

The first thing I usually do to the lead vocal at mix time is to patch in a compressor. Since I usually record the lead vocal with some compression (just enough to get it to "fit" on the tape), I usually don't need to add very much more. (By the way, when you record vocals, be careful about overcompressing. You can easily add compression at mix time, but it's not possible to remove it once it's on the tape.) There are a few ways to approach this job, and you'll simply have to try them all several times before you find out what works for you.

Method number one is to use very heavy compression (8:1 or more) that the vocal hits only at the loudest peaks. This is not a very subtle way to do it; you'll definitely hear the compressor working, but in some situations it works well. Method two is to use a very low compression ratio (2:1 or less) with a low threshold. The compressor will always be working, but with a minimal depth.

Method three is between the previous two extremes, and it's the method I usually use. I set the threshold so that the compressor is active about half the time, and I use a medium (3:1 or 4:1) ratio. Since I usually don't want to hear the compression, I also use the "soft-knee" curve. Bear in mind that the results you get will vary, depending on the compressor you are using—they each sound different. Some are great for some voices and terrible for others. Some are great for drums and not much else. Some don't sound good on anything at all! I've even had occasions when two of the same model compressors from the same manufacturer sounded quite different from each other. You'll have to make adjustments for each situation you come up against. Just use your ears; that's what they're for.

A little experimentation is crucial in setting a compressor properly, so don't be afraid to use the technique of listening to too little and too much compression with the threshold set too high and too low. After awhile, you'll get the hang of it.

Lead-Vocal EQ

As you set the compressor, you can also play with the eq. If the voice is too muddy, try taking out some lower midrange, or boosting some highs. Use as little eq as possible—if you've adjusted every knob on a four-band eq, you've probably messed up. Try starting over with the controls flat. Once again, there are so many variables involved—Who is the singer? Which mic was used? What do the surrounding instruments in the track sound like?—that it is impossible to give specific recommendations on how to set the eq. You'll have to work it out on your own. I can tell you that there will come times when you've gotten the voice to sound great on its own, yet it gets lost in the track. Very often, this means that the surrounding instruments occupy the same sonic territory as the voice. Try soloing the lead vocal with each instrument in various combinations. If you're lucky, you'll find that only one or two of the support instruments are really doing the fighting. If the problem is caused by sequenced instruments, like drums or keyboards, you can simply change sounds until you find more compatible ones. If the conflicting instruments are on tape, you've got another problem entirely. Try panning the offending instruments away from the voice and turning them down a bit. If this doesn't quite do the job, you'll have to do some corrective eq to the clashing instruments. Listen to the sound of the voice with the sound of the instruments, and use the eq to take out the areas where the sounds overlap. A very common clash for me is between electric guitars and male rock singers, particularly if the guitars are distorted and the singer has a raspy voice. If you've got to deal with this situation, try cutting the guitars at around 1 kHz.

Lead-Vocal Effects and Level

The vocal effects you choose will make or break the character of the voice. I almost always use reverb, as do most producers. I very often use delays, setting a slap (100 to 250 ms) and/or a rhythmic delay. Sometimes I use a mono-in stereo-out pitch transposer set to a very slight detune (1 cent sharp on the left, 1 cent flat on the right) for thickening. As you try these and other effects, you'll develop a sense of what you prefer.

Once you've set the compresser and eq and decided on the effects you want to use, you'll need to set the vocal level. One thing I've found is that if the vocal is loud, the mix can be listened to at a low volume. This is not always a good thing. For this reason, I usually mix the voice loud enough to be understood, but low enough to encourage the listener to crank it a bit.

Don't Forget to

Take a Break
Your ears will become tired after a fairly short period in front of the monitors; after an hour, your ears are fatigued, and you won't hear as well as you did when you started. It helps to take an ear break of ten minutes every hour or so. When you take your break, leave the studio! Go outside and get some air. Relax.

Change Your Listening Perspective
In addition to gross ear fatigue, it's easy to become numb to your listening position. Every once in awhile, take a listen to the mix one room away from the studio. You may notice some items that need adjusting—things you had gotten used to when sitting in one spot for awhile. Be careful about the balance of the bass instruments. Remember that the closer you get to a wall or corner, the louder the bass will appear to be.

Do Lots of Mixes
Unless you're mixing to ¼″ 2-track, you can afford to do lots of mixes. (Hopefully you aren't mixing to cassette.) After all you've spent on equipment and studio time, you're practicing false economy by trying to save on mixdown tape. Since the advent of DAT, it's now possible and reasonable to do ten or more mixes—just keep some basic notes detailing the changes you make to each mix, or use the slate function on your mixer. How do you "slate" a mix? Simple. If your board has a talkback mic, you simply send it to the main outputs. When you press the talkback switch, the mic's output will be sent to the mixdown recorder. Before each mix, you explain what's going on. For example, "This is take four of [your song's name here]; we've added a bit of bass, and we're going to run the solo a little quieter." If your mixer doesn't have a talkback feature, or if the talkback can't be routed to the main record output, you

can simply set up a mic and run it through the channel. It won't need to be very loud at all—just so that later on you'll be able to tell what you said.

However many mixes you do, be sure that you do some track-only mixes, which can come in awfully handy later on. Suppose someone else wants to do a demo of your song. If the key is compatible, they can use your track mix by recording it onto two channels of a multitrack, leaving several empty tracks to cut vocals to. Mixing the new version will be a snap, compared to doing a full mix. Track mixes are also useful for TV performances, or even live gigs. If your song has lots of big backing vocals, you may want to make a couple of track mixes—one with no vocals at all and one with no lead vocal but with backing vocals.

Mix in Pieces

Sometimes it's impossible to do an entire mix all the way through. Even with two people helping, there are so many moves that there's no way to make them all without heavy-duty automation. There's an option that's been used for almost as long as there has been tape recording: editing. The idea is that you splice together all the good bits into one good mix. A big advantage of mixing in pieces and then editing is that you can set up entirely different reverbs and other effects for each section—effects that would be difficult to change in the middle of a mix.

The tricks involved in this process are making sure that you've got all the pieces you'll need, and planning where your edit points will be. By the way, it's best to have plenty of "overlap" between the pieces, in case your planned edit points don't work.

The Ideal Mix

For me, the ideal mix is one that has emotion to it, like any other performance. Even if there are some minor technical problems, such as a backing vocal that didn't get turned up enough, I tend to prefer a mix that felt good as I was doing it—I believe these mixes feel better than the technically perfect ones.

I also prefer to *listen* as I mix, rather than get too caught up making move after move, hoping that the last one worked out as I reach for the next. For this reason, I use *lots* of automation. Home-studio automation is slow—it takes lots of patience and skill to use it, but the beauty of it is that very fine adjustments can be made from mix to mix. Want the solo to come in a shade louder? Simple: Type in a new controller value in your sequencer. Want the reverb to "swell" at the end of the bridge? Assign a MIDI controller to the reverb level (I'm assuming you're using a reverb that allows MIDI manipulation), and start the song with a level of 80 or so and swell it to 127 (the maximum MIDI controller value) at the end of the bridge. Once this move is written in your sequence, it will repeat every time.

Even though I use MIDI muting to comp vocal tracks, I generally run the vocal-level moves by hand — "milking" the vocal or the vocal's effects at certain lines or moments. Once you develop the knack for it, this is a great way to enhance the lead vocal's emotion, as well as the emotion of the entire mix.

MAKING COPIES

Make copies of your mix and store them in different locations. That way, if you should lose your master (either by accident or by natural disaster) you'll be able to quickly replace it. If your mixes were done on DAT, it's easy to make digital copies that are vitually indistinguishable from the master. If your mixes are on 2-track open-reel tape, make copies on DAT.

When you send out tapes, make the effort to have them sound and look their best. This is no time to skimp — if you've taken the time to make a great demo, don't ruin it by sending out lousy copies. Making great cassettes is easier than you think: Simply use great tape on a great machine, then label them in a professional fashion. If you're going to buy a new cassette machine, buy the one that makes the best-sounding copies; in fact, take along a favorite CD to record when you go cassette-machine shopping. I suggest that you avoid features like auto-reverse and auto-timer, since they don't add sound quality and they cost more. Also, avoid the dual-cassette "dubbing" machines — they generally make really poor copies. If you must make copies from a cassette, use two good cassette machines instead. When you make copies, use Cr02 (Chromium Dioxide — type II) tape and *no noise reduction*.

If you can afford it, a three-head cassette machine is the best way to go. It won't necessarily sound any better than a two-head machine (all other things being equal), but the three-head machine will be easier to set levels, since you'll be able to monitor off the tape itself as you record. A two-head machine will monitor its input only as it records, so you need to rewind and listen back to see if the tape sounds OK.

Once your tape sounds great, make it look great by labeling it properly. Here's the information every tape should have: the titles of the songs, a copyright notice, and your name and phone number. If you have too many songs on a tape to list them all on the label, you can call the tape "437 songs by . . .," although if you are submitting songs to a publisher or record company, you should send no more than three or four songs. If they want more, they'll call you — as long as you've put your name and phone number on the cassette label. As far as copyright notice goes, I usually put the following: "© 199 — by Hank Linderman, All Rights Reserved."

Warning: I am not an expert on copyright law, so I am not suggesting that you follow my example. I do suggest that you contact AS-CAP or BMI for copyright information, or purchase a book that deals more with the business of music before you settle on a copyright notice procedure.

If your handwriting is exceptionally neat, it might be OK to label your cassettes by hand, but it is best to use a printed label. If you have a computer and a printer, you can generate labels of your own. Failing that, go to a printer and get labels made.

It is becoming more common to send out DAT tapes as demos rather than cassettes. The reasons are obvious — your tape will sound better, since DAT machines are much more accurate in terms of sound quality and tape speed, whereas no two cassette machines seem to sound the same. Also, DATs may be more likely to get attention, since there are usually fewer DATs being received than cassettes. The down side is that DATs cost more, and very few people have DAT machines in their cars (where lots of listening gets done). It's your choice!

THE LIVE DEMO

One of the best ways to record a song is to do it the old-fashioned way — live. There are lots of advantages: speed, economy, fun, and the wonderful feeling of a good, live performance. If you're a songwriter and a performer, making live demos can be a great way of finding out if you've really "finished" the song or to help decide whether or not to do a full demo. Great songs work with just a voice and a guitar (or piano); there's no production to hide behind. Since most home studios don't allow the use of live drums (not to mention an entire band), I'm limiting my definition of *live demo* to minimal accompaniment—a main instrument or two (guitar/piano) and a voice. Once you get comfortable with this sort of approach, try adding a bass, percussion, more voices, etc.

Live to Two Tracks

It may be tempting to record live to your multitrack, but that leaves open the all-too-tempting possibility of overdubs, as well as requiring that you mix. Go directly to 2-track. DAT is best, since the tape costs are minimal. This is important, as you will see.

Set Up Your Mix

Here is the one drag of live to 2-track: You have to make a mix as you record, and this mix often has to serve as the headphone mix for the players. Everything may sound great in the phones, but on playback, the lead vocal is *way* too loud. The way to work this out is to do several test passes of the song and play back the results until you're happy. The players may have to make some mental adjustments in order to achieve the proper balance. The good news is that since there are relatively few sonic elements to deal with, the mental adjustments shouldn't be too difficult. If there are two singers, I usually use one mic and make the singers adjust their relative balance by moving into or away from the mic. If one of the singers can't hear well enough, have him remove one side of the phones so he can listen to what's happening in the room. For guitars or pianos, I usually use a separate mic for each instrument and make adjustments at the board, while electronic instruments can go direct. The more instruments there are, the more difficult the mix will be, so make things easier and keep it simple.

Be Ready to Do Lots of Takes

Once you've got your mix, just start running the tape and record take after take after take. Maybe you'll get a stellar peformance on take one, but don't be surprised if it takes several more. If you're recording to DAT, be sure you're using a long tape—one hour at least—and once you start rolling, don't stop! If you make a mistake, just count off again and start over. Once you have the take you want, copy it over to your master reel. The tape you started recording on can be used again for something else.

Move Quickly

Although you should be ready to do lots of takes, try to be finished recording within an hour. By keeping the pace of work up, you limit the amount of analyzing that can be done by the performers, and analysis is the enemy of the live demo. (Someone once said, ". . . analysis presumes a cadaver. . . .")

Performance Tips

Since it's going to take some experimentation to get the mix you need, save yourself (performance-wise) for later. You'll get all the takes you need, so start slowly and build, one take at a time. Keep the pressure low and attitudes relaxed.

Very often, you'll find that a performance that feels great sounds awful. I can't tell you how often I would be on stage for a set that was magic for me, only to be asked on break if there was something wrong. The converse has also happened—I feel like I'm struggling and get congratulated by a listener. The point is this: Evaluate the takes *after* they've been recorded—don't worry about it when you're putting them down.

I've noticed a performance pattern in lots of singers and players: The performance after a "peak" performance is often a very weak one. I think this is totally normal, and the weak performance is often a clue that the previous one was indeed the peak. If you get to the point where the peak performance still isn't good enough, take a break of a few minutes before you try again. Let the performers clear their minds—talk about anything but the song. Even after the break, it will be difficult to surpass the previous peak, so don't worry if it doesn't happen. You can always try again a few days later.

PART THREE

FINAL THOUGHTS

PRACTICAL CONSIDERATIONS

Here are some suggestions that will help keep your demo-recording process running smoothly. I'll tell you in advance that I don't always follow my own advice on these practical matters, but I should!

Keeping Track of Your Tracks

Once you've done a few dozen demos, you'll be at the point where your memory isn't enough to keep track of what songs are on each tape, what's on each track of each song, or which effects were used in the mixdown. For this reason, it's a good idea to keep records of what you've done with each song. The best place to start is with a track sheet. Here's an example:

BASS GUITAR	12-STRING GUITAR	ACOUSTIC	GUITARS	TAPE _1_
1	2	3	4	SONG _1_
ELECTRIC	PIANO	DISTORTED ELECTRIC GUITAR	CLEAN ELECTRIC GUITAR	SMPTE _0:00:05:00_
5	6	7	8	MIDI FILE _NEW SONG_
LEAD VOCAL	DOUBLE	BACKUP	VOCALS	
9	10	11	12	
WORK	TRACKS	GUITAR SOLO	SMPTE	
13	14	15	16	

Track Sheet

As you can see, I simply printed up a grid and labeled it for the number of tracks I'm using (sixteen), along with some basic information regarding which reel of tape it is, which song, what the SMPTE start time is, and the name of the MIDI sequence file.

One thing I've found is that it helps to have a more-or-less standard track layout—not that I *always* do things the same, but that I save time and mental calories by consistently using the same tracks for the same instruments. This lets me mix faster, since I already know where the instruments are. I usually put the bass on track one and SMPTE on track sixteen, since both of these signals tend to leak to adjacent tracks—this arrangement means that these signals will leak to only one track each rather than two. (The highest- and lowest-numbered tracks are "edge" tracks.) On analog machines, all signals "leak" from their track to their neighbors—this is called *crosstalk*. Bass frequencies leak more easily, and SMPTE is such an unmusical sound that any leakage can be a problem. Also, SMPTE tracks are sensitive to crosstalk from neighboring tracks, particularly from rhythmic signals, which can cause sync problems for your sequencer. If I need to use the track next to the SMPTE track, I make sure not to use it for a rhythmic part—like drums. Lead guitar is much better suited, since leakage from SMPTE won't be heard because of the guitar's high level on tape, and the SMPTE will generally be unperturbed by the guitar. (Digital multitracks have essentially no crosstalk, so bass and SMPTE can be put on any track you wish.)

I usually print lead vocals on tracks nine and ten, backup vocals (bounced from other tracks) on tracks eleven and twelve, and MIDI work tracks on tracks thirteen and fourteen. Guitars and other played instruments go on tracks two through eight. I use the back of the track sheet for general notes, such as lists of what still needs to be done and effects suggestions for the mix. Once the mix is done, I can also note any special settings I want to be able to recall. I store the track sheets in the tape box, and I also label the outside of the tape box with the titles of the songs on the tape. All this makes keeping your tapes organized lots easier.

Maintenance

There are some important chores regarding your equipment that simply must be done in order to keep your studio running trouble-free. The first is to keep all your machines and instruments clean and free of dust. You can use a feather duster on a daily basis to clean your mixer, keyboards, tape machines, computer, etc.—all those devices that are dust magnets. Every week or so, use a vacuum cleaner (turn your equipment *off*) for a more complete dust removal, and every month you can use a slightly moistened towel to clean up any smudges and finger residue. Don't use cleaning solvents—water only. (Be sure to check your owner's manuals for proper cleaning procedures.)

Your analog multitrack tape machine requires more specific care.

You must clean the heads with a cotton swab and cleaning fluid (100 percent denatured alcohol, which has no lanolin or other oils, or specialized tape-head cleaning solution, available from your tape machine's manufacturer) *every* time you use it. If you don't, the machine will give less than stellar performance, and you may even cause damage to your machine and your tapes. The pinch roller (that big rubber wheel that holds the tape against the capstan, which pulls the tape through the tape path) also needs to be maintained. There are special rubber cleaners you can use that help to keep the pinch roller clean and conditioned, counteracting the effects of air pollution and age. I have found this rubber cleaner and conditioner only through Teac/Tascam dealers. *Never* use alcohol on the rubber pinch roller, and *never* use the rubber cleaner on your heads. Ask your dealer if you need help.

Another job you should do each time you get ready to record is to demagnetize the heads on your multitrack machine. This is a tricky job, requiring a special tool (called interestingly, a *tape-head demagnetizer*, which you can get for under fifty dollars at your dealer). As you use your multitrack recorder, the process of pulling tape through the tape path causes any metal parts to become slightly magnetized. If this magnetism is allowed to build up over time, it will become powerful enough to cause a loss of high frequencies on any recordings you make, and it may even cause partial erasure of tapes that were previously recorded. This damage is not repairable. When you use the head demagnetizer, you wipe away any of this residual magnetism. There are several precautions you must follow:

Clear away any tapes. The demagnetizer is a magnet, and it will erase any tapes that are close by. This includes cassettes and multitrack tapes—put 'em away.

Your machine must be turned *off.* Turn off your machine even before you turn on the head demagnetizer. If you don't, you will cause permanent damage to your tape heads, and they will need to be replaced. Tape heads are very expensive.

Be sure the demagnetizer is at least four feet away from your machine before you turn it on. When the demagnetizer is turned on, it can cause an electromagnetic "spike," which can cause permanent damage to your heads.

Move the demagnetizer slowly, but keep it moving at all times. If you move the demagnetizer too quickly, you can cause permanent damage to your heads. A speed of one inch per second should be your maximum. *Never* stop moving a demagnetizer that is turned on. (If you do, you can cause permanent damage to your heads.)

Once you've started, don't stop until you're finished. Here's how the actual procedure goes: Clean the tape machine (with cotton swabs and cleaning fluid), then hold the demagnetizer at least four feet away from your machine (which is *turned off*), and turn the demagnetizer on. Slowly, move the demagnetizer toward the heads on the machine, starting at one end. Move the demagnetizer (slowly — up and down in ½" movements) over each metal part (without actually touching them) of the tape path — the tape heads, guides, lifters; these are the pieces that become magnetized. When you've covered the entire path, begin to slowly pull the demagnetizer away from the machine, still moving it either up and down or side to side as you pull it away. Once the demagnetizer is four feet or more away from the machine, you can switch it off. Mission accomplished.

Another caveat: If you mess up your tape machine or tapes by using a tape-head demagnetizer improperly, it's your problem, not mine. Your machine may have different requirements, so it is your responsibility to find out what the proper procedure is. Consult your owner's manual, talk with your dealer, or call the manufacturer for help.

Backing Up

Since much of what goes on in a home studio involves a computer, it's very important that you have copies (backups) of the information you use. Sequences, sounds, lyrics, contracts, programs — all of these need to be backed up to avoid disaster when your computer's hard disk crashes. Notice that I said "when" your hard disk crashes — it *will* crash someday, and the better prepared you are, the easier your recovery will be. Make at least one copy of everything and keep it on floppy disks. Current work needs to be backed up frequently. How frequently? Ask yourself, "How much work do I mind redoing if my system crashes?" The answer to that question will tell you how often to back up.

Your mixes need to be backed up also. If you mix to DAT, you can simply borrow another DAT machine and make copies of all your mixes. Once you've made the copies, store them in a different location, such as a relative's house or a safe-deposit box. If there is a fire (God forbid) at your studio, at least you'll still have your mixes.

Equipment can be replaced—all it takes is money. Your mixes are irreplaceable.

When Disaster Strikes

Sooner or later, you will be the victim of some technical disaster. Machines will fail to work, software bugs will appear out of nowhere, files will be deleted, tracks will be accidentally erased—all of these are normal occurrences. When disaster strikes, try to remain calm. You may be tempted to: (A) scream and curse; (B) become violent; (C) become despondent; (D) all of the above, capped off with a crying fit. None of these scenarios will help your situation, so find some serenity, or at least fake it. When disaster strikes, you'll need some help. This is where your network of fellow demo producers, music store salespeople, computer nerds (yes, I am a computer nerd) and manufacturer's service representatives come in. In my situation, when I have a Macintosh problem, I call a few of my Mac friends. When I have a PC problem, I call a friend who is a real wizard with PCs. When I have a software problem, I call others who use the same software or the manufacturer directly. When one of my machines goes down, I call the music store I bought the machine from, or the manufacturer. (Here's a tip regarding technical support from manufacturers: Be sure you know what you're talking about before you get a service representative on the phone. If you're a beginner, get help from the store or a friend. If you've become more of a power user, you'll probably be able to get help only from the manufacturer. Look in the back of your manual for the manufacturer's phone number, call them, and ask for "technical support" for the product you need help with. Try to be near the uncooperative machine and have the manual and serial number handy. Most often, you'll be asked to leave your name and number so that the tech can call you back.)

Of course, it helps to study your manuals, but you must also be prepared for the possibility that the manual is wrong. On several occasions, I have called a manufacturer to let them know of bugs that I have found in their newest product. Just last week, I called a manufacturer with problems I was having with a new digital tape machine, only to be told that the "recommended" tape I had used was now "definitely not recommended."

Sometimes the disaster requires very creative thinking to work around, such as when a machine has apparently functioned properly but has in fact made a mess of the work you are doing. The more experienced you are and the more experienced help you have will make all the difference in the world in how you rectify the situation. Remember: Seek out experts!

When all else fails, you'll simply have to redo the work you've lost because of machine malfunction. Stay relaxed — it happens to everyone — and get the work redone as quickly and painlessly as possible. So much of the work in demo production is going down blind alleys, so don't get discouraged when it happens to you.

YOUR ULTIMATE TOOLS

Ask a musician what her most important tools are, and you'll likely get a variety of answers: "my '65 Strat," or "my Steinway." A singer might go so far as to say "my voice." I say these answers are off base.

Of all the things I've written about in this book, what I have to say now is by far the most important, and it's also the easiest to ignore. All you have to do is to pretend that what I'm talking about couldn't happen to you.

I'm talking about the ultimate tools of our trade — our ears.

Have you ever played the game of "if I had to give up one of my scenes, I'd give up. . . ."? What about the opposite game; in other words, which sense would you least like to lose? For me the answer is easy. My hearing is my most treasured sense.

The hearing problems of Pete Townshend have been public knowledge for several years now. Every story about the Who tour of 1989 mentioned it. Pete was one my of major heroes, and reading about his hearing loss and tinnitus (ringing in the ears) left me saddened and vaguely disturbed.

Then my own hearing problems began.

Late in the spring of 1990, I began noticing that ear fatigue induced by long sessions wasn't going away by morning. If I took an extra day off, my ears would settle somewhat, but I never got back to what I would call a completely normal state. At this point, my fatigue was a minor annoyance. I kept on working.

Maybe it was because I was using headphones; maybe it was the long hours — in any case, my ear fatigue worsened. Within a few weeks, my ears were physically hurting. I began to be more sensitive to sound — any sound. My ears were ringing steadily, just a little, but steadily nonetheless. The ache in my ears was constant. I kept on working.

There's a well-deserved respect in the music business (or any business) for determination. Sheer determination will take you farther than you can imagine. I don't remember now which song I was working on at this point, but I was determined not to be slowed down by mere physical discomfort. I felt somewhat noble pursuing my muse even in the face of disaster.

My ears were unaware of how noble all of this was. They got worse. Now my earache was extreme. The ringing in my ears had become a factor to be considered when I was recording. I had become so sensitive to sound that simply dropping a fork into the silverware drawer triggered even louder ringing and ear fatigue that I could only previously have attained by hours at a very loud concert. I began to wear earplugs constantly, even while sleeping. Earplugs only made life bearable.

One of the Circles of Hell in Dante's *Inferno* is where the punishment is the heightening of one's senses to the point of excruciating pain. My ears were certainly at that point. Any sound at all was painful. I almost got into a fistfight with an announcer outside a movie theater who pointed his megaphone at me as he announced upcoming showtimes and ticket availability. Didn't he know how much pain he was causing me?

I went to an ear specialist. I got my hearing checked and had a physical exam of my ears. None of this took very long. The news was not good. I already had a measurable loss in both ears—more in my left ear.

Hearing loss is irreversible.

The hypersensitivity to sound was caused by excess pressure in my inner ears. I got a prescription to help circulation in my ears and was told to cut salt out of my diet. (Salt increases blood pressure.)

It took several weeks for me to feel any real relief. The ringing in my ears was driving me crazy and leaving me despondent. One of my friends mentioned that there have been cases of mental illness induced by tinnitus. No kidding.

Relief did come. You cannot imagine how hard it was to give up salt, but it was worth it. The pain in my ears backed off a bit, as did the ringing. I could walk around without earplugs. Life had meaning again. It was late summer, and my ears had been ringing nonstop for about four months.

I had never really stopped working, but I had made some changes. I stopped using my "big" monitors (Yamaha NS-10s) and began to rely almost totally on a little pair of Auratones. I used headphones only while singing, and kept the level as low as I could stand it. I started taking ear breaks every hour or so.

It is now several years later. My ears still ring. My ears still hurt. I'm still a bit oversensitive to sound. At this point, my ear problems are bearable. I feel lucky, and yet on the edge, as though my hearing were in constant danger of a relapse.

The point I'm trying to make is simple. Your hearing is in danger, just by being a musician. You have two choices: Tell yourself that it won't happen to you and go on about your business, or examine the way that you work and consider any changes that might be necessary. Look for any warning signs, and pay attention when they occur. Get your ears tested, even if you don't think you have any hearing problems. Don't kid yourself, because the bad fact is that what happened to me could happen to you.

So keep working, but *turn it down*.

INDEX

More Great Books
for Songwriters!

1995 Songwriter's Market—Find out where and how to sell your songs with 2,500 updated listings of music publishers, record companies, booking agents, and more—750 of which are brand new. Plus, you'll find information on the business of songwriting, the hottest trends, plus listings of songwriter organizations, contests, competitions, and workshops. *#10386/$21.99/522 pages*

The Songwriter's Market Guide to Song & Demo Submission Formats—Get your foot in the door with knock-out query letters, slick demo presentation, and the best advice for dealing with music publishers, record companies, producers, managers, booking agents, and advertising or commercial music firms. Plus, you'll get information on fine arts organizations, contests, and more! *#10401/$19.95/160 pages*

Creating Melodies—You'll be singing all the way to the bank when you discover the secret to creating memorable melodies—from love ballads to commercial jingles! *#10400/$18.95/144 pages*

Who Wrote That Song?—If you're a music buff, you'll love the 12,000 songs listed here—everything from mid-nineteenth century ballads to today's Top Forty hits, with emphasis on the last forty years. Each listing includes title, composer, lyricist, and publication year. Where appropriate, listings also reveal who made the song popular, others who recorded it, and who sang it on Broadway or in the movies. *#10403/$19.95/432 pages/paperback*

Networking in the Music Business—Who you know can either make (or break) your music career. Discover how to make and capitalize on the contacts you need to succeed. *#10365/$17.95/128 pages/paperback*

Beginning Songwriter's Answer Book—This newly revised and updated resource answers the questions most asked by beginning songwriters and gives you the know-how to get started in the music business. *#10376/$16.95/128 pages/paperback*

Songwriter's Idea Book—You'll find 40 proven songwriting strategies sure to spark your creativity in this innovative handbook. Plus, learn how to use your unique personality to develop a strong writing style. *#10320/$17.95/240 pages*

The Craft of Lyric Writing—You'll get a complete guide on writing words for and to music, choosing song formats, and writing lyrics with universal appeal from bestselling author and songwriter Sheila Davis. *#01148/$21.95/350 pages*

Making Money in the Music Business—Cash-in on scores of ways to make a profitable living with your musical talent (no matter where you live). This guide covers performing as a solo or in a group, writing music for the radio, jingles and more! *#10174/$18.95/180 pages/paperback*

Successful Lyric Writing—Write the kinds of lyrics that dazzle music executives with this hands-on course in writing. Dozens of exercises and demonstrations let you put what you've learned into practice! *#10015/$19.95/292 pages/paperback*

Songwriters on Songwriting—You'll share in the triumphs, disappointments, and success secrets of 32 of the world's greatest songwriters as they candidly discuss their art. *#10219/$17.95/196 pages/paperback*

The Songwriter's Workshop—With this tape and book workshop, you'll discover how to write lyrics, make a demo, understand MIDI, pitch songs, and more! Plus get loads of inspiration and creativity sparkers. *#10220/$24.95/86 pages plus 2 cassettes*

Music Publishing: A Songwriter's Guide—Get a handle on your songwriting career! This practical guide gives you advice you need on types of royalties, subpublishing, songwriter options in publishing and more! *#10195/$18.95/144 pages/paperback*

88 Songwriting Wrongs and How to Right Them—Avoid the common pitfalls that swallow many songwriters with this indispensable trouble-shooter's guide. You'll find expert instruction on how to fix what's wrong with your song. #10287/$17.95/ 144 pages/paperback

You Can Write Great Lyrics — You'll write songs that have what it takes to succeed with this one-of-a-kind guide. It covers what works in the industry and how to understand its ups and downs. #10120/$17.95/184 pages/paperback

Stage Lighting Revealed: A Design and Execution Handbook — This all-in-one guide will answer your lighting questions whether you're a beginner or an experienced designer or electrician. You'll learn the functions of equipment, how to create special effects, pre-production, and much more! #70201/$14.95/176 paperback/ pages

1995 Poet's Market — This new edition has over 1,700 listings — complete with expanded submission information! You'll get invaluable information on the business of poetry, enlightening poetry samples, upfront articles and interviews with successful poets and editors, plus a complete section of poetry conferences and workshops. #10388/$21.99/552 pages

The Art and Craft of Poetry — Nurture your poetry-writing skills with inspiration and insight from the masters of the past and present. From idea generation to methods of expression, you'll find everything you need to create well-crafted poetry! #10392/$19.95/352 pages

Creating Poetry — Definitions, examples, and hands-on exercises show you how to use language text, subject matter, free and measured verse, imagery, and metaphor to create your own wonderful works! #10209/$18.95/224 pages

The Poet's Handbook — Get expert instruction on how to use figurative language, symbols, and concrete images; how to tune the ear to sound relationships; the requirements for lyric, narrative, dramatic, didactic, and satirical poetry and more! #1836/$12.95/224 pages/paperback

Writing Articles From the Heart: How to Write & Sell Your Life Experiences — Holmes gives you heartfelt advice and inspiration on how to get your personal essay onto the page. You'll discover how to craft a story to meet your needs, and those of your readers. #10352/$16.95/176 pages

Writing As a Road to Self-Discovery — Add depth and dimension to your writing through a series of directed exercises designed to help you explore what has shaped you, what has hurt you, and inspired you. Then Lane helps you transform the answers into "your story." #10370/$16.95/208 pages